Enjoy our beautiful U.P. of Michigan.

Amy J. Van Ooyen

LIVE IT U.P.

by Amy J. Van Ooyen

To: Dave, Enjoy!

Published by:
"The Woodpecker Books" Press
N13508 Partridge Rd.
Ironwood, MI 49938

First Printing May 1991
Second Printing June 1991
Third Printing April 1992
Fourth Printing September 1994
Fifth Printing June 1996

Printed by:
EERDMANS PRINTING CO.
231 Jefferson S.E.
Grand Rapids,Michigan 49503
(616)451-0763
Fax (616)459-4356

To Claude

The Illustrations in this book
were drawn by Amy Van Ooyen - Greving, (authors daughter).
Amy is a freelance Illustrator and Graphic Designer
living in Grandville, Michigan

FOREWORD

There aren't many good books about the Upper Peninsula of Michigan that capture its tough people and wild beauty but here's one that does so. Reading it brought me back home again.

Incredibly the book was written by Amy Van Ooyen who had not spoken a word of English until emigrating from Holland, at the age of 29, shortly after World War II to settle in Grand Rapids. Amy is the mother of eleven children, the last four of whom were adopted from Korea after Amy became a board member of the Holt Adoption Agency, an international organization. She traveled widely arranging other adoptions, had tea with the Queen of Siam, got tangled in the jungles of the Philippines, and drove a school bus for fifteen years to help put her children through college.

During their summer vacations the Van Ooyen tribe did a lot of camping and spent much time exploring the U.P. Like so many others they fell in love with the land and its people and upon retirement headed north again, this time to stay.

This book is the story of the Van Ooyens' life in the woods near Lake Superior but it is much more too because Amy has included marvelous little tales about the people who came to their back door, tales of beekeeping, goats, woodcarving, fishing, and making it through the winter. Amy is a born story teller and her book is fun to read.

But don't give it to your summer visitors. They might not go back Down Below.

.......Cully Gage
(Dr. Charles VanRiper)

Table of Contents

EEL LAKE CABIN

"Someday we will buy land," Claude promised, "a small parcel that will be ours."

We were crossing the long bridge that spans the Straits of Mackinaw toward Michigan's lower peninsula, returning home from a month-long camping vacation in the U.P., and I had wiped away a tear. "Air pollution," I told the children. "Late August is hay fever time."

The children were eagerly looking forward to seeing their friends again, tired of travel and camping in remote forest campgrounds. "I'm lonesome for Cindy," Alvin said. Cindy was the neighbor's dog.

I never grew lonesome for anything downstate. I wiped another tear, blew my nose, and reflected on Claude's idle promise. Buy land in the U.P.? Impossible. A crazy idea of my husband, the impractical optimist. I knew he was hoping to console me. He didn't buy that hayfever thing.

Buy land? Where would we get the money? We had eleven children; seven in college and high school, four in grade school. That made for a tight budget! Claude worked many hours overtime to support the family, which cost more and more every year.

I looked sideways at his serious face, smiled through my tears and squeezed his hand. "Sure," I said, "We'll buy land. Some day." But I didn't believe it.

For fifteen years we had vacationed in the U.P. Its forests, lakes, waterfalls, and Lake Superior's rocky shores and sandy beaches were part of our lives.

"Why must we always go up north?" the children would ask, but Claude and I would never hear them. We loved the U.P. vacations and built trips around a variety of interests. One year we focused on waterfalls, another year on traveling the shore of Lake Superior. One summer we explored the history of mining. And of course, we always looked for the best fishing spots or canoe routes where we might discover wildlife. For Claude and me, Michigan's Upper

Peninsula was everything.

Then one day it happened, and we found ourselves driving 500 miles north from our home near Grand Rapids to a secluded part of the Ottawa National Forest near Marenisco. Friends from the U.P. had phoned. A lake cabin in the National Forest was for sale. They warned us that the cabin needed repair, but knowing our love for the area, they felt we might be interested. "We think the owner will sell if we come along as references," they said.

It was early May. In the U.P. spring comes late, so we drove cautiously, watching for deer that feed on spring grass sprouting between patches of snow. As we neared Watersmeet, a deer suddenly bounded in our path, bounced off the bumper, and disappeared in the forest. The car continued to purr, but then we heard a loud hiss. We limped into the only gas station and motel for miles around and took a room to await morning.

While trying to rest, I thought about our dream of a cabin in the forest near a lake. It had seemed an impossible dream, but we had nurtured it for years and shared it with friends. Now it seemed the dream could become reality.

In the morning, the gas station repairman examined our car and found it had been punctured by the fan due to the impact of the deer. "I'll get a neighbor to drive you to your friends at Langford Lake," he said. "Don't worry. Your car will be ready this afternoon."

At Langford Lake we met our friends and drove in their car to Eel Lake at the end of a winding, narrow road in the Ottawa National Forest. There we found the cottage of our dreams, we, a man and woman from Holland.

The owner had not arrived, and we looked out over the lake, musing. "How did I get to this place in the wilderness of the U.P.?" I asked myself. A pair of loons drifted lazily in the sunlight. What made us leave the safety of dikes that kept back the North Sea and move to the United States of America?

Why did we leave the confinement of an overpopulated country? Could it have been the same hunger for freedom to roam and explore that now made me want to buy an old cedar log cabin?

I walked out on the old crumbling dock. A small yellow perch lay parallel to the dock like a miniature torpedo, its fins pumping the rhythm of fish life. "Grow up, little fish," I said. "We'll be neighbors next summer, just wait and see!" Bulrushes and cattails growing sparsely along the shore rustled their approval.

Claude joined me on the dock. "What did you say?" he asked.

"Claude, I want this little cabin, and I just told the fish so."

Eel Lake Cabin

"I want it too," Claude said.

"Is it bad to want something so very much?" I asked.

"It depends. We'll wait until the owner comes. What's her name?"

"Mary, Mary Young. She is selling the cabin because the Forest Service ordered her to make expensive repairs. Is it possible that we could buy it?"

I hoped Claude would say yes, although I knew he seldom gave a direct yes or no. Always I get just a cautious, indirect answer.

"The walls are sturdy," he said.

I looked up toward the cabin built of vertical cedar logs, now black and mildewed by many harsh U.P. winters. I didn't know why I wanted the small cabin so desperately, but I did. With all my heart I desired those white birch reaching for sunlight and the soft green balsams and cedars. I wanted the glittering lake and that little fish, when it grew up. I wanted all of it!

Suddenly cheap blaring music shattered the quiet. From behind the trees a little lady approached. She wore a bright red pant suit and carried a pocket radio. Chattering above the music, she explained that she had come along the lake shore to avoid the hill behind the cabin.

11

"Where is my Loon?" she asked. Have you seen my papa Loon? Where are you? Yoohoo!" she yodeled. A western pop tune from a radio strapped to her wrist clashed with all the nature around us. She did not introduce herself, but we knew she must be Mary Young, owner of the cabin.

Constantly jabbering, Mary showed us a huge ring with dozens of keys. "I had some extra made for you folks," she said, "three of each. This one is for the front door, this one for the back. That little one is for the boat, and this one must be for the outhouse. We have a key for the gasoline can too. My husband built this cabin, but he is gone. We don't understand why, but he died on Christmas Day, didn't he Gladys?"

Only then did we notice Gladys. She was thin and seemed to be wasting away from some disease. Dressed in black, she was almost invisible, a small shadow following Mary.

"I'm Gladys," she said, snatching a puff from her cigarette. She gave us a sad smile and coughed.

"Gladys is my sister-in-law," Mary said. She chattered on cheerfully. "Her husband died too, so we live in my house. Do you like my cabin? Deany, my husband, was not well when he tried to repair the roof."

Suddenly she looked helpless. "The Forest Service keeps reminding me that I must fix this place, and because I can't, I have to sell it. My Deany was so happy here. He built it in 1950."

She talked and talked, repeating herself, while we waited. The keys rattled and Mary's twittering disturbed the peace, but not the cabin! Its cedar logs formed a stronghold against Mary's onslaughts. She tried to find the key for the door. Claude asked kindly if he could help but received only a vague answer. "This must be the right key. No, that one. No?" Reluctantly, she let Claude try, and he soon opened the door.

Mary entered first. Pointing proudly to the door she said, "See the claw marks? Bear. You must be careful here, you know. Bears come at dusk, so keep the door locked."

The fresh forest air gave way to the musty smell of wet, molding clothes, mothballs, and mouse urine. No! I thought, This horrible, stinking place is not fit for living.

Holes the size of a man's fist near the chimney opened up to the sky. Firewood in the old wood box sprouted mushrooms. It was evident that rain and snow had kept this cabin damp for years. Mary found a handful of sawdust behind a day bed. "You naughty carpenter ants are back," she said. "Gladys, do we have any Raid here?"

The other woman had not followed us inside, but I heard her cough and utter a strangled no.

The ceiling of imitation wood-grain cardboard exposed three squirrel nests with strips of cedar and cotton protruding from gaping holes. No, this dank dungeon is not for us, I thought.

Feeling almost nauseated, I fled to the lake, wondering if the view from the dock had been a mirage. The wail of a Loon echoed across the silver water as the bird raised high, stretching his wings to claim the lake for himself and his mate. The perch was still there. "I'm crazy, but I want this place," I said stubbornly. Some cottage!

As I stood on the dock, I could hear Mary Young talking a torrent, a never-ending stream of words. Claude's deep voice stated with quiet persistence his evaluation of costs and materials needed for repairs.

Looking at the dilapidated building and remembering the stench, I smiled, "A summer home?" Then noticing Gladys who had folded her body like a sick bird at the rotting picnic table, I joined her. She smiled, coughed, and waited quiet and dignified. Steps muffled by humus and pine needles made me look up. It was Claude. He came to give me his verdict.

We walked toward the dock. "Do you still like this place, Amy?"

"Will it forever smell like that?" I asked, needing encouragement, My dream was fading fast!

"The building is solid," Claude said. "It sits on a firm foundation. The floor is not bad, except near the chimney where it is rotting. The roof will need work, but it looks worse that it really is. I can fix the building, but you will have to do the rest."

"Will we tell Mary we'll buy her cabin?" I asked.

"Not unless she'll stop talking!" he answered. Then he said thoughtfully. "Can we afford it? She is asking $1200."

"No," I said. "We can't. But we'll manage. All our children will pitch in and enjoy this place. We'll move in with the mice and squirrels and with the porcupine that lives under the floor of the

13

outhouse and the bats that raise a family between the posts and the paneling on the east wall."

"Well, you'll never be lonesome here," Claude teased, "loving wild creatures like you do."

I nodded. "Let's buy it."

Claude exchanged a down payment check with Mary Young for all her keys. Sensing her loss, for a moment she stopped talking. Then she began again to tell us of her husband Deany who had built the cabin and how he had loved this place so much. Understanding that her dream would never end and that it would always be Deany's cabin, Claude gave her the extra key to the front door and invited her to come often for a visit.

We watched the little old lady in the red pantsuit disappear among the green balsam, Gladys following, still quiet and barely visible. We heard the radio fading, and in the distance a loon laughed, freeing us of our guilt for having bought someone else's dream with cash.

OUR CHILDREN COME

Wrestling and pushing, yelling and shouting, five teenage kids ran to the top of the hill. I saw their arms swinging and heard their feet pounding on the springy forest path, then I heard a series of splashes. Our children had found the lake.

Knowing it would be a disaster to come to our unrepaired cabin in the evening, we had camped near the Presque Isle Flowage on M64. The following morning we drove to Eel Lake to find that a late June frost had shriveled the maple and black ash leaves. And we found that our little log cabin had become part of nature. Pillows of green moss covered the leaky old roof. "The roof will last our life time," Claude had assured me on our first visit. I hoped so!

Claude called the children to come, but they couldn't hear his voice above their clamor, so I tried our camping call, "Yeeeuhoo!"

We heard a faint, "Coming!"

Ellie 15, Amy 14, Calvin and John 13, and Alvin 12 raced up the hill dripping wet, shivering, and jabbering at the same time. " Open up! Dad. Do you know what key it is? Why so many keys for this little place?"

Claude found the right key and the door creaked open. The children crowded in, a bundle of bare arms and legs.

"Phew!" one said.

"Horrible. It stinks!" echoed another.

"Mom, Mom; do we have to <u>sleep </u>here?" Ellie's big brown eyes pleaded with me.

"Not like it is now," I replied. "We'll clean it up.

There is another door at the other end of the cabin. Dad will open it and we'll all pick up stuff to throw away."

"You first, Dad," Amy said, with a grand sweeping gesture. Claude took the former owner, Mary Young's, flannel bathrobe from a nail and tried it for size. Then he walked out into the bright sunshine. I donned an old helmet, a relic from Dean Young's army days, and marched out to the old picnic table. The spirit caught on.

15

Dean Young's breeches held two boys, one in each leg, as Cal and Al tumbled out the door.

We took inventory of the cabin. The boys gathered fishing equipment, hardware and old sports magazines. We girls carried out dishes, silverware, bedding, and linens. Everything smelled horrible from dampness and neglect. We sorted and discarded, setting aside things to be washed.

An hour later, we looked around a very empty cabin. The floor was bare. A beautiful row of toadstools decorated the wall near the chimney, straight up to the old red stones. The studs holding up rough masonry against the logs were green with a slimy mold, and the three squirrel nests we had observed on our first visit still protruded through the holes in the ceiling.

Lunch time came, but our young crew was determined to tear the stained, rotting Linoleum from the floor. "Dad! Mom! look!" they shouted. "Come see the nice boards!"

I was heating pork and beans and making sandwiches, but I paused to look. The wide pine floor planks were streaked with white mold but still solid. It was a beautiful floor, except for rotting planks near the chimney.

Claude assessed the roof then looked at the walls separating a small bedroom from the main room. "That must go," he said. "I'll build two double bunks and add another window to give us more light."

Before lunch, the crew swept the cabin clean of spider webs, mouse nests, and what else mice leave behind. We discovered that Mary Young had her private inventory system. An ammonia bottle held vinegar. Cooking oil was kept in a ketchup bottle and dish soap in a window cleaner squirt bottle. Our daughter Amy was totally confused by a label on an empty container of bouillon cubes that said "mink oil."

"Don't worry," Cal said, "Mom won't poison us!"

But I did not trust myself. "Before we eat mink oil soup throw that out with the other junk," I ordered.

We assigned the boys to wash the dishes and silverware on the dock. Standing half naked in the water, one washed, one rinsed, and the other splashed. They accepted the otherwise detestable job. "The sun will sterilize them;" I said, "boys, dishes, and all."

16

Eleanor and Amy drove with me to the laundromat in town. They helped me carry in baskets and bags of laundry then disappeared, unwilling to admit that the foul-smelling articles were ours. They deserted their mother in her hour of need!

I explained to all who would listen that this was not our regular wash, that we had just bought an old cabin. The other patrons did not seem to care much, but the stench overpowered even the perfumed soap. At just the right time, the girls returned, offering me a candy bar and begging forgiveness. They helped fold the linens and were amazed to find the sheets, blankets, towels, and pillow cases smelling fresh.

With cunning and scraps of board, Claude finished one double bunk by nightfall. So with the bunk, the couch, and a mattress on the floor, we prepared to occupy our new residence in the U.P. We carried tables, chairs, and other furnishings inside. It is unbelievable, I thought, what seven pairs of willing hands can do in so short a time.

Though the air swarmed with mosquitoes, we chose to eat outside near the campfire, blending our evening devotions with a robin's song and a bullfrog croaking his love to his mate. Then we took our Saturday evening bath in the lake, covered by nothing but the evening darkness.

Claude and I watched for awhile, our gratitude almost matching the starlit expanse above. "Our children soon will be young adults," Claude said.

"Yes," I answered. "Three or four years, and they will leave us, like the other six, then Eel Lake will be quiet again."

During the night we heard scratchy noises as little forest creatures tried to reclaim their territory, carefully studying the destruction of their domain. But we were tired and slept deeply.

A loon woke us early Sunday morning, his shrill tremolo calling to his mate. Looking out of the window, I saw her swim past with her baby tucked securely on her back. It was a bright, cold, North Country morning, fresh and clean with the smell of evergreens.

We planned to attend eleven o'clock worship at Bethel Lutheran Church of Presque Isle. Getting ready was just like home, a confusion of rushing and squabbling. The girls hogged Mary Young's full-length mirror on the inside of the front door. The boys fussed with their hair.

"Why are girls always so privileged?" they complained. "They stand for hours in front of a mirror. We only want a minute to comb our hair."

"Run over the hill to the car," I ordered, to get them from under foot. "It has three mirrors, one for each of you." They stomped up the hill muttering, "Why do we have to go to church, anyway? It spoils the day."

"We will go to church," I said to myself, "because we have reason to worship. We will say thanks to God today."

Climbing the hill to the car in the cold morning air, the sun warmed us briefly, but still we shivered in our light jackets and sweaters. Our car was too small for a family of seven. Like hens on a roost, the children shuffled each other for space. And there was a definite pecking order. The most aggressive chicken found a spot between Claude and me.

The girls complained, wanting the windows closed. The boys wanted them open, claiming they were being asphyxiated by their sister's perfume.

"Your hair is touching my face, Ellie."

"Mom, John is wiggling his butt again!"

"Quiet!" Claude warned, "or I'll stop!"

"Mom, she is pinching me now."

"Is this the way we give thanks to God?" I asked myself. "Surely there must be a better way." But I too was frustrated. "Grow up!" I shouted, as I had to that little fish months before. "But not yet," I prayed, "Not too fast."

The seven-mile ride was worth all the fighting. We found a little church with brown cedar siding built on a peninsula between two walleye ponds. As we approached, we heard an organ playing a prelude. Large evergreens lining the driveway swayed their heavy branches in the morning breeze.

Inside, the church was light and cozy. A dozen people waited for the pastor. Our eyes were drawn to the stained glass window behind the altar. It portrayed Christ's disciples hauling in a net filled with fish. Fish! Eel Lake fish!

A bouquet of lilacs decorated the organ, and a larger one graced the altar. Late for the season, I thought, forgetting last night's frost.

Our children reverently followed us in, sensing that this was God's house. They settled quietly next to us in the pew.

The organ began the first hymn and the pastor entered. Before he began reading the familiar old liturgy, he turned to us. "I am Pastor Weber." He smiled and blew on his hands to warm them. "It is cold in church this morning. We don't have heat because a robin has chosen God's house to build her nest. She made it on top our chimney. Rather than disturb her, we worship in a cold church, but with warm hearts!"

Blowing again on his hands, he gave us a blessing. "God bless you and keep you; in the name of the Father, the Son, and the Holy Spirit." The organ responded, leading us into a joyous "Amen."

A short sermon followed the liturgy. Pastor Weber spoke about how each of us had received special talents. He told of a friend in the area, an expert trout fisherman. His special talent was preparing the fish and sharing them with others. May we so share God's love with our friends, Pastor Weber concluded. Amen.

We received another blessing from his uplifted hands. We shivered, but our hearts were warmed. I shuffled toward the door remembering a text, "Even a sparrow has found a home, and a swallow a nest for herself, where she may have her young, a place near your altar, O Lord, My God."

As we left for home, a robin sang from the evergreens. I was reminded of an old Dutch hymn learned fifty years earlier in Holland, and I sang the words, which were unfamiliar to my children here in America.

Beneath Thy care the sparrow
Finds place for peaceful rest.
To keep her young in safety,
The swallow builds her nest.
Then, Lord, my King Almighty,
Thy love will shelter me.
Beside Thy holy altar,
My dwelling place must be.

I don't think the old Eel Lake cabin ever experienced so much fun or enjoyed more attention than came to it that weekend. We scrubbed it from top to bottom, although the smell of mold, dead mice, and dirt still lingered.

Ellie had an idea, "Why don't we varnish the logs?"

"Yes," Amy added, "And we could paint the floor bright red and the window frames green, but the outside must stay as it is, weathered and brown."

We all agreed. The varnish covered the bad odor, painting the floor also helped. At last, the shiny floor looked bright and almost new. The girls, unable to quit painting, carried the old chairs outside and soon they matched the floor. With the paint that was left, we covered the porch planks.

Later, we bought red-checkered oilcloth for the table and cupboard shelves, and white valances to decorate the windows.

Meanwhile, Claude had inspected the roof and was surprised to find a trowel, hammer and a large can of roofing tar behind the chimney. It was as though Dean Young was pleading, "Please fix my place. I tried but could not finish the job."

We worked hard, but we took time off for fishing, hiking, and canoe trips with friends who camped at the boat landing a mile from our cabin. One morning, the boys were out rowing on the lake. We saw them hurrying back. "We saw a huge fish! Maybe we can catch it in our big net."

I remembered seeing a man trolling past our dock early one morning. Later, he was searching, as though he had lost something in the lake. When Calvin returned huffing and puffing under the weight of a large musky, I guessed what had happened. The unlucky fisherman had lost his fish, his propeller probably cutting his line and injuring the musky. The fish Cal carried measured 38 inches, and it had a wide gash along its back.

Cal still holds the record for the biggest fish from our lake, but we had other contests--one for bass, which I won. The boys still claim it was pure luck, not skill; but near shore one day, on my first cast, I hooked a 24-inch bass and claimed the $5.00 prize.

The problem was, we did not have five dollars so I had to pretend, which was even more fun. All of us were skilled at pretending.

Money was often a problem. We did not have enough cash for a roll of asphalt to fix the roof on the lake side, so Claude made temporary repairs with sheet plastic and Dean Young's tar. When it rained hard, we used Mary Young's camp kettles, pretending the tickety-tock was pleasant, yet hoping the rain would stop.

Our second Sunday at Eel Lake was warm. Claude and I watched our children playing and teasing each other at the dock, the boys splashing the girls, who were sunning on a blanket. Ellie, as always, reading; Amy sketching the shore line; Claude, grumbling that the boys were too rough with each other; it was a normal, pleasant day.

Suddenly, we heard a familiar, disturbing sound. We recognized it as Mary Young's pocket radio! Helplessly, Claude looked at me. "Nothing is free," he said.

Mary yodeled above the loud country music, "Yoohooo! Loon where are you? Here is Mary. Are you home, little loon?"

Dressed in bright blue with a red hat, she followed the path and heard our children. Climbing the steps, she lifted her short arms, the radio blaring from her wrist, "Oh Deany, aren't you happy? Do you see these beautiful children? And so many!"

"Sit down, Mary," I said. Will you turn down the radio a little?"

"No, No!" she answered. "I must go see your children." Chattering, she walked to the dock.

Gladys, her companion came quietly from the woods carrying a large round cake pan in both hands. She placed it carefully on the picnic table, then sat down as if exhausted and reached for her cigarettes.

Mary, bubbling and noisy, returned with all five kids. "We'll have a party!" she announced. "I made a chocolate cake. Gladys, where is the cake? Oh, here it is. We'll have a tea party! Make us some tea, Amy. Deany loved chocolate cake with lots of frosting!"

Ellie came to help me in the cabin. "Mom, I don't remember what Mary told me to say to you."

"You don't have to give her an answer." I replied. "Just say yes once in awhile. She is a nice lady. Why don't you kids eat your cake near the lake?"

As we had our party at the picnic table, Mary observed the red painted porch floor. She talked aimlessly. At intervals we answered,

21

"Yes, Mary." Finally, I broke in. "Would you like to see the cabin, Mary?"

She hesitated. "No, I'll stay here with Gladys."

Gladys looked tired. "Would you like to rest on the couch for awhile?" I asked. She nodded and smiled gratefully.

I turned to Mary. "Would you like a boat ride? The boys will row. Maybe you will see the baby loon." I called Calvin and John. "Don't use the motor, take turns rowing, and be careful!"

Mary was elated. "It must be more than ten years since I was on the lake," she said. "And now two gentlemen will be rowing the boat."

The boys were polite to the little woman. Faintly, we could hear her jabbering and Calvin's changing young voice giving assurance.

"Peace," Claude said. "Dean Young must have loved her a lot, and he loved this cabin, too. I'm sure of that."

Finally Mary returned, feeling happy. "I love you all! I will come often." Tense and a little shy, she looked toward the cabin.

"Gladys is resting inside," I said. "Won't you come in?"

Slowly, Mary followed me inside, and Gladys sat up. "It's nice and clean, Mary, so cozy!" Her eyes, questioning, sought Mary's.

"It smells different," Mary said, almost angrily. Then she looked up at the deer mount, a buck with a perfectly symmetrical eight-point rack. "That is Deany's trophy, he was so proud of it. I'm glad you didn't throw it away."

"We'll keep it here always in memory of Deany," I told her. "And we want to thank you for this cabin. You must visit often. You have a key? Use the cabin as though it were still yours!"

"I'm glad you and the children enjoy Deany's cabin," Mary replied. "Yes, I have a key, and I will come often."

But she did not use the key. Mary never returned.

IF YOU THINK YOU DON'T HAVE FRIENDS, OWN A CABIN NEAR A LAKE

 My young artist friend Carol wrote these word on a slab of wood. She had captured the scenic view of our old cabin resting against the hill between balsam, birch and cedar trees. Gifted with an eye for beauty and nature's wonders, Carol's artistic talent is unspoiled. In childlike faith, she paints lovingly, accepting God's world with unconditional trust.

Carol was right! Our summer days were like beads on a string with one visiting friend leading to another. Some visited for a few hours, some for a day, while others pitched a tent, camping among the trees close to the lake.

John and Ardy, friends from Down Below (anywhere south of the U.P.), came with their three children in an old school bus converted into a camper. The turn-around space on our dead-end forest lane served as their campground. Happily singing, that family of five skipped some steps as they descended the hill to our cabin shouting "Surprise!" They joked about the wild secluded area we had chosen to live during summer.

Those five were tall and wiry, all resembling each other. Like the five birch trees near our dock, they shared their roots and supported each other. John and Ardy laugh, sing, and have fun. And were fantastic fishermen. Their two boys were also dedicated to the sport but their daughter Lynn despising live bait (or pretending to, as teenage girls do) had much more in common with our girls.

Spending one evening singing around our campfire, we made plans for the next day. We decided on an all-day fishing trip to the Presque Isle flowage for us fishermen. The Presque Isle is now controlled by a dam and is a relatively undiscovered treasure, with wild life in abundance and good fishing.

Early the next morning, Claude went to town for supplies while I estimated the appetites of eight teenagers and four adults to plan the day's menu. Would five pancakes each be enough? Probably not. I added another dozen. Eggs were in short supply; we'd have those scrambled. Lunch would be easy: peanut butter and jelly sandwiches, carrot sticks, gallons of Koolaid, and hot coffee for the grown-ups.

Supper was more difficult. The girls had planned a hike. Claude would be working on the cabin. And we, the fishermen, might be late, possibly returning after dark. Stew, I thought, a large kettle of thick stew and a quick salad. Then anyone could eat when hungry.

Placing Mary Young's big kettle between two frying pans on the three-burner stove, I turned the flap-jacks in short order. That little gas stove must have been an invention of the late 18th century, worth a fortune to an antique dealer. But it worked!

Opening the door for better ventilation, my eye caught a fast-moving black animal. Why was our black dog Julie walking so funny? I wondered. Not quite sure, I glanced through the window toward the lake. It was not Julie! A two-year-old bear stretched herself full length in front of the cabin, playfully rolling on her back. Then, with a clumsy gesture, she reached for Julie's two month old puppy.

The bear must have been lonely after her mother had ousted her, and so was our puppy, the last of Julie's family. So they rubbed noses. Julie arrived, smelled danger, and barked at the bear, snatching her pup and directing him to hide under the cabin.

The disappointed little bear wiggled its short tail and stumbled to the porch, smelling food. But there she met a new adventure. Mouche, our cat, was nursing her kittens. The awful stare of Mouche stopped the bear. When she nosed curiously into the kitten's box she was attacked by a hissing, spitting ball of fur. Hastily retreating and licking her sore nose, the bear left, waddling sadly to the hill. The bear had not meant any harm, I almost felt sorry for her.

"What was that noise, Mom? Why was Julie barking?" The sleeping bags in the bunks were moving. A head popped up like a turtle from its shell.

"A little bear came to visit," I said. "It is time to get up!"

"A bear. Aw Mom, you're fooling," one answered. "A new trick to make us get up."

Another smart kid added, "Can't you do better than that, Mom?"

"Yes, for sure!" I replied. How about a cup of cold water!"

One by one they reluctantly slipped from the sleeping bag, leaving their cocoons limp.

Our guests running single-file sang their way down the hill where the bear had gone up! "Breakfast is ready, I called. "Did you meet that bear?"

"What bear? Amy. You're fooling, of course," John laughed.

Ardy noticed the stacks of hotcakes. "No boys, not yet! I'll go for my camera and make a picture first."

"Watch out for that bear, Ardy," John teased.

She did not meet the bear, but it made for good conversation, and the food disappeared, leaving not a scrap for a little friendly bear.

"Mom, that was too obvious," Amy scolded.

Ellie, a year older, said, "Can't you be more original, Mom?"

Changing the topic, I tried to organize our day and fishing trip. John offered his large boat to all. "No," I protested. "You and Ardy and the boys use that. Our John and I can take the small boat, while Calvin and Alvin use the canoe. We'll leave them at the Teal canoe landing and meet for lunch near the first duck blind."

I knew John and his family would stay on the water unconcerned about storms, lightning, or the rain that the sultry dog day promised. Soon the heavens were splitting open, with lightning and hail hurling down. Perhaps it doesn't occur to John that lightning could strike him dead out there in the boat, or maybe he does but doesn't care, but I planned to hide on shore.

My son John and I fish well together, concentrating seriously and enjoying the sport. John and Ardy and boys sing, swing their poles, and are happy-go- lucky fisherman. The day went well. Big thunderheads rumbled past us in the north over Lake Superior, threatening, but not coming closer. And the fishing was very good.

It was almost dark when we climbed the steps of the hill, Ardy singing "by the light of the silvery moon." Then "Whoops!" and Ardy stopped. "I hear a noise!"

Some twigs snapped. We listened. Yes, I heard it too, a soft grrr.

"Oh John, help, it's the bear!" Ardy shouted and ran toward to the cabin. John dropped his stringer of large northern pike at my feet and was gone.

I froze, then I heard a soft giggle and relaxed, my heart still aching. More twigs snapped and someone said, "We scared them good. Where is Dad? Mom is in the cabin!"

Two figures walked up to me. This was the last strew. "Never mind," I said. "That is where you should be. You girls are reckless. We did have a bear here this morning."

Ellie and her friend giggled, "We waited for an hour! Are you all right Mom?" I did not answer.

Ardy was safe in the cabin now and John entering the back door sat down at the long table built for twelve. The stew, tasting like it should after a ten-hour cooking time was devoured. We had fish stories and tales of bears for dessert. Ardy gave another rendition of "Silvery Moon."

Calvin and Alvin told the story of Big Max, a bear caught in a trap at a forest campground. "Mom was so worried the bear would escape. It banged all night long on the trap."

John once more had to ask, "But your bear here is friendly, right Amy?"

"Yes it is. You did not have to run, John," I said. "But be careful now when you go to your camper."

Claude always is up first in the morning, making a pot of coffee and taking a dip in the lake. Very surprised and dripping wet, he met the friendly little bear walking sideways down the hill. "Hey, we do have a bear here!" he shouted, running for the door.

"Is it friendly?" I asked. "And does it want to play?" I turned comfortably in the now-roomy bed and waited for Claude to bring me a cup of coffee. Julie barked furiously and woke the rest of the house.

"A bear? Where, Dad? Let me see it!"

"No, me first!"

A mess of arms and legs blocked the door. "There is a real bear, Mom!" one shouted.

"Oh yeah," I said. "You must be fooling and trying to get me out of bed. Take a cool swim."

"Mom, it's true, we have a bear here!"

Claude, now convinced of danger, suggested, "Maybe I should go to the D.N.R. and ask them to set a trap today. There might be

26

more."

John and Ardy called, "What's for breakfast?"

"Only cereal and boiled eggs, but we had a lot of excitement here. The children will tell you we had a friendly bear here," I replied.

"So it was no joke?" John asked. "Well, why don't we fish this lake now and we'll leave for Manistique later today. We want to fish for the huge blue gill and walleye near Curtis. What do you think, Ardy?"

By mid-afternoon our guests were gone and the D.N.R. officer set his trap at their camping site. The next morning we found our friendly little bear waiting to be released. It begged for help, rolled on its back, and was very pleased with Alvin tickling its belly with a stick.

"We will release it in the Porcupine Mountains," the officer promised. "There it will have enough space to grow up to be a big smart bear."

The loons now were silent because their chick was mature, no longer needing protection. There were mornings when flocks of ten or twelve loons visited near our dock. Several times our family had cheered the chick as it tried to fly. Our high hills presented a challenge for the loons, forcing them to circle the lake twice before gaining enough altitude to soar above the trees.

Our loon chick had failed every day, disappointing us. Then on Labor Day at early dawn, I watched the bird. Once more it began its long noisy run, became airborne and flew higher and higher before returning to our dock for a second try. Again it became airborne and we heard the morning air pumping through the slow, even, wing strokes. We watched as the young loon proudly flew over the trees and out of sight.

Now it was our turn to go home, and I understood. One by one our teenagers must learn to fly. They may fail at first and come home to rest, and then they will try again.

OUR HOME IN THE WOODS

"We think Mom has spring fever!" the children told Claude one evening early in March.

"You mean she's ready to go fishing?" he asked. My rod and reel were waiting for me in the corner of our bedroom.

Yes, spring had arrived, and as usual it had the children worried, for they knew that spring meant the annual spring cleaning rite. Hoping their father might think of some way to escape the danger, they looked to him for help. Counting Dad with the kids, it was eight to one, but they all knew I would win in the end and everyone would be drafted to do their part in cleaning the house from attic to cellar. Walls were to be washed, floors waxed, and worst of all, closets organized until Mom's spring fever had run its course. Then she could go fishing.

Sometimes, when I was lucky, March gave us one of those wonderful sticky snowstorms which canceled schools for a day. I made good use of these snow days! We found lost scissors and pens, unreturned library books, and jewelry that the girls had accused each other of losing. Even a dollar bill was retrieved from its hiding place. But best of all, socks separated for months found a patiently waiting mate and were reunited. In the end all were happy, knowing it would be another year before Mom would have another attack of spring fever, as my daughter Amy called it.

But those hectic days were soon forgotten as we anticipated spring vacation and a trip to our Eel Lake cabin in the U.P. Not wanting to waste any time, we left right after school was out one Friday afternoon in late March. We drove across the Mackinaw bridge at night, admiring the mighty structure illuminated against the dark sky.

Leaving early in the morning for the western part of the U.P., we reached the National Forest road that led to our cabin by late afternoon.. A snowstorm the day before had transformed the woods into a fairyland, perfect for skiing to the cabin waiting for us five miles down the road.

Reluctant to be first to desecrate the white sculptured beauty, we decided to take turns, but the children pushed ahead of Claude and me. Taking a short cut across Eel Lake, they found the hidden key and started a fire in the cabin.

In no hurry we followed the longer forest trail to the steps that led over the hill. Climbing slowly we carried our

Our Home

skis and sank deep when we missed a step hidden by the snow.

From the top of the hill, the scene was exactly as we dreamed it would be during that long winter. The small cottage lay hidden under the evergreens, mostly balsams, their snow-laden branches folded like an umbrella, patiently waiting for spring to relieve their burden.

With all my heart I again said Yes to this place. If only we could live here permanently!

The days of that early vacation were filled with cross country skiing, exploring the nearby lakes, reading, and playing games. Dean Young's old sports magazines dating from 1950 and Mary's old magazines with old-fashioned hair styles and clothes gave our teenage girls bursts of hysterical laughter.

Having to melt snow for cooking water, our coffee tasted somewhat herbal. Perhaps fine evergreen needles added the unexpected flavor. Clean snow mixed with Koolaid and sugar made delicious snow cones for the kids. Birds and animals came for a hand out, appreciating our leftover scraps.

A week later skiing back to our car we seemed almost to have lost track of days. On the windshield a slip of paper told us that we had been recognized by the friendly folks in nearby Marinesco. "Welcome, don't get lost!" the note said. Another note added, "See you in spring!"

Savoring the warmth of being welcome, we left the forest behind and drove to Ironwood for the second reason of our vacation trip. Friends had informed us that forty acres of wooded land were for sale north of Ironwood. The property was located near Lake Superior, five miles from Little Girl's Point. Following the Realtor's directions, we came to a two- track road that lead to a hunting camp built on the forty- acre parcel.

The children, skeptical but adventurous, stared at the old building covered with imitation asphalt siding, its door swinging sadly in the wind.

"Oh no! Is this where we are going to live?" one asked. "It's worse than Eel Lake cabin!"

"Will we be poor when Dad retires?" Ellie said, looking at me with a worried expression.

"I don't like this place!" echoed Amy after her sister.

Claude calmly quieted the group. "We're just looking, not buying. Not yet, anyway."

I was not so sure. I knew he liked these private woods a half-mile from the main road and ten miles from town. Questioning my own courage for a lifestyle so far from neighbors, I had my doubts.

"Here's an outhouse, but some animal ate part of it!" Alvin shouted.

"Oh, porcupines; they'll eat anything. They like salt," Calvin informed us. "I read about it, Dad. Even the tires of your car aren't safe." It was plain he hoped to discourage Claude from buying this place. My husband did not answer Calvin.

"The price is much too high," Claude said, thoughtfully inspecting the cabin. "It's not very well built." He looked at me, expecting an answer.

"Where will we go to school? What is there to do?" the children asked over and over.

Remembering our adequate home in Grandville, I said, "Don't worry!" But I lied to myself. I was worrying.

Returning to town, we left the children at McDonalds, assuring the hungry teenagers that hamburgers and french fries were still available a short drive from the woods. Then Claude and I went to the Realtor and made an offer, just half of what he had asked for the property.

The children felt quite secure, believing we would never move them to those Upper Peninsula woods. While Claude wished the offer would be accepted, I was caught, as often had happened before, somewhere in between.

But during our first week back home, a telephone call settled the matter. The Realtor told us the owner had "reluctantly" accepted our offer and he would close the deal upon the arrival of our check. So that was how we became owners of forty acres and another old cabin, this one near Lake Superior.

Our four married children were even less enthusiastic about the new property than were the younger ones. They reminded us we were getting older. "Your friends move to condominiums to retire," they said. "They all go to a warmer climate. You will freeze up there! And it's too far away! We will miss you too much."

Their arguments could not persuade us to change our decision. We were not going to retire just yet. In the years to come, our five younger children needed an education like the older ones had enjoyed.

Our eldest son Peter was more optimistic. "Our parents are different," he told the girls. "They are naturalists, and a rugged lifestyle would suit them."

One evening Peter told his father that he'd found a job opening in Vancouver, Canada. "If I take that teaching position," he said. "I'll have three summer months of free time. Would you like to have me build you a home this summer up there in the woods?"

Claude liked the idea! and plans quickly materialized.

"Mom, I'd love to build a log home for you," Peter lamented, "but it is to be a frame structure, 24' by 36'. Any other specifications?"

Yes, build the house without walls in the interior except for the two bedrooms and a bathroom. And I would like a loft with an open stairway."

Surprised, Peter showed me his sketch. He had laid out the space exactly as I had specified. He had designed the house with a cathedral ceiling. I was pleased. It looked spacious!

The forest crowded the east side of the house, and when Peter asked, "Mom, I'll add a deck to the house. What size would you like it to be?" I laughed.

"A deck! For what, Pete?"

"For you and dad to sit and have coffee," he answered.

"And look at the woods?" I asked. A deck seemed absurd and I began to cry.

"Mom?" Peter asked.

"Oh forget it I told him, this is so big an adventure. You boys work so hard just for dad and me. We can't ever reward you. Besides I'm not really sure this is what I want, living here in these strange woods. This will take all the money we have plus more we must borrow."

"Mother you're missing dad. You always loved to live in the U.P. Its just your attitude. Be happy! We don't mind all the hard work for you and dad. You did so much for us.

I dried my tears and looked up to our six foot four son who now lectured and gave me comfort. We had immigrated once, and then I did not know the language of our country. At least I could communicate with U.P. citizens, and yes, Peter was right; I loved to live here where I was close to nature.

The small two track road leading off Lake Road about five miles east of Little Girls Point was too isolated for a power line, and the cost prohibitive at this point. The constant booming of a generator told me the location of our home going up in nowhere, when I ventured out to explore the dense forty acres.

First the foundation was dug out. The basement walls were only five feet high because of the high water level. Then a friend built a fireplace. The bare chimney pointing to the sky was an awkward sight. Peter told me, "It's like an arm stretching out to help him build our home around that towering structure."

The mason friend who built it had only that one week to do so, but he did!

The cathedral ceiling and the walls were plastered, with cedar battens, which were to be stained mahogany brown. That was my job. Standing on the makeshift scaffold, I tried to keep my balance physically as well as mentally. Peter kept calling, "Mom don't smear the white plaster. You're shaking too much!"

"I'm no steeple jack," I told him.

The work was finished in three weeks of hard labor by all of us. I was more proficient as camp cook than staining in high places, cooking five meals every day, with snacks in between, and ran to the spring often for ice cold water. The temperatures were 80 to 90 degrees daily, and the boys drank gallons of lemonade and Koolaid.

At last we took pictures of the workmen and the house then left for home.

In 1976 we spent another happy spring vacation at Eel Lake and visiting our new house in the woods. Before we left for home, Calvin looked up at the skeleton of rafters inside. "I'm still tired," he said, remembering the long days of hard work.

A short visit with Mary Young ended the full week of fun. She chattered, babbled, and busily told us, "Gladys is gone! I don't know what happened, but she died suddenly in January. I'm the only survivor of the family now, and I will come to see you at Eel Lake and in your new home, too."

Without expecting a reply, she kept cheerfully explaining about her faith which does not allow for age, sickness or death. Mary believed in a loving God who gives only health and happiness. We left Mary talking more to herself than to us.

That summer, Peter, with the help of Calvin and John, completed our home, It was not yet time for retirement, because Amy and Ellie were attending college now and the three boys were in high school. We occupied the house only a few weeks in the summer of '77, alternating with fun days at the Eel Lake cabin.

My brother and his wife from the Netherlands vacationed with us that year. It was impossible for them to understand that we owned so much land. "An estate!" they called the forty acres. Compared with the crowded lifestyle in Europe, we seemed wealthy, and for us not to occupy our new house seemed to them a waste.

Claude and I spent the Labor day week-end at our Eel Lake cabin, and on the last beautiful Sunday afternoon before we were to go home, we estimated the expense of educating four children in college the next year.

"We'll never be able to retire," I complained. Bursting out in despair I added, "But if we finally do, we must promise God to share our home in the woods with others. Anyone will be welcome, anytime!"

Claude did not answer. He is more reserved and used to my impulsive moods. Angry at his reaction, I shouted "But I will never give this cabin to God!"

For a few minutes it was very quiet. Then we were surprised to hear soft muffled steps as a young man walked out of the woods and came down the hill. "I'm John Anderson," he said. "I live at White Pine. We've been looking for a cottage. My three boys like to hunt and fish. Someone told me you might be willing to sell this place because you had built another house and were a little short on cash."

"What?!" I said. "Sell the cabin because we're short on cash? Never! How did you find us? Who told you? We don't owe anyone a cent!"

Furious and with tears burning my eyes I ran to the dock, full of rage. That man could not have come at a worse moment. How could we sell Eel Lake cabin, the only place where I had found rest and peace? No, he could not pay what this place meant to me! Just to know it was here waiting for me anytime I wanted it was enough to make life downstate worthwhile.

Hearing Claude asking questions made it worse. Why should he give that man even a chance? The two men walked toward the dock, Mr. Anderson telling my husband how convenient his family would find this location for an evening of fishing.

"What would you ask?" he concluded, sounding impatient.

"Can you give me a price?"

"Amy, why don't we talk this over in private? Excuse us," Claude said.

Fighting tears, I heard Claude say, "Amy, you must be reasonable! We certainly can use the money, and we don't have to sell unless he gives us a good price. What do you think of five thousand dollars?"

"I don't want to sell the cabin. I don't! But if we must, go ahead!" I answered.

Stubborn and mad I fled again, this time up the hill. I paused to catch my breath at the foot of the steps and angrily snatched up a scrap of paper. Littering! People always throw trash. I hate it, this is God's country.

I looked at the wrinkled, soiled paper in my hand and noticed that it came from a daily devotional publication. The heading was barely legible. "June 3," it read. "Facing a crisis with courage," I read on. "A Christian often faces a crisis. You may run, or trust God and remain true. You will be better prepared for the test of future storms. At times a Christian must confront a crisis head on, by faith. So move forward."

How did this paper get to our steps? Today was September 2. Numbly, I walked to the end of the lake. Standing there, I wished there were no God. I would win this battle! No, I was not going to give up my cabin, my special hiding place.

"God, I can't and I won't! But if this is God's country, as I had so often said, then it is not mine.

Returning slowly to the foot of the steps, I gave the cabin back to God.

There was no great sense of victory, neither relief or tears. It hurt too much. I found Claude and John Anderson near the picnic table. They had come to an agreement. The cabin would be sold for thirty-five hundred dollars pending approval of Anderson's father-in-law. They exchanged telephone numbers and John Anderson left, promising to call in a few days.

We never heard from him again.

That soiled piece of paper rests in my pocketbook with our credit cards. It gives us free use of Eel Lake cabin as long as God gives us credit.

In the summer of 1978 we moved to our home in the woods. Our house downstate in Grandville sold for five thousand more than we had expected, and with Claude's retirement our children became eligible for grants, scholarships, and loans. We have kept our promise to God to share our house in the woods, and at times we have had some unusual guests!

I was surprised there were so many visitors who found our secluded home. Resting awhile they usually traveled on, but some became friends who returned every year.

Melba Rigoni

VISITORS

"Happy birthday to you! Happy birthday, happy birthday!" Cheerful children's voices rang through the quiet woods from behind the young balsams lining our driveway.

Surprised, my goat Barbara leaped forward, dragging me along on her tether. Since her four legs work much faster than my two, I was pulled unwillingly to the barn, where Barbara sought safety from noisy kids and the biting flies.

Barbara is the most important female on our property. She is greatly admired by our visitors, and she has posed with more famous people and has been more often photographed than many of Hollywood's sexiest stars. Barbara is a charmer; fluttering eyelashes hide her evil thoughts and she grins an innocent, toothless smile.

The melody coming from our driveway upset not only Barbara, but our squirrel Halftail, who lives at the bottom of the squirrel totem pole. He escaped from a hawk one summer day, leaving half his tail behind. Now, half a tail was not much of a meal for the hawk, but its loss led the squirrel into shame. His short tail offers Halftail no protection on rainy days, as a full tail does for his relatives. When it rains, Halftail runs around in his underwear to the chatter and laughter of his friends. But we like him, and only Halftail among all the squirrels near our home gets peanut butter crackers. He lives among the gnarled roots of our old hemlock, a tired old tree that stands with dignity close to our door. Halftail and the hemlock welcome all visitors who come to our woodland home.

And visitors come, some of them a bit peculiar, so I was not too surprised when a Cadillac halted under the hemlock. Having recovered from my adventure with Barbara, I approached the car and found an elderly couple listening to the babble of children's voices on a cassette player; the source, I concluded, of the children's voices I had heard.

The couple were in tears, the lady repeating, "Dear me, Oh dear me, dear me." The man behind the steering wheel blew his nose and swabbed the tears streaming down his face.

Concerned, I asked, "May I help you? Perhaps you would like to come inside for a while."

The lady shook her head sadly. "My husband has difficulty walking, but yes, we would love to visit with you." She began to weep again.

"My husband is home," I said, "I will call him. I summoned Claude from his workshop and told him of our sad visitors. "We must help these people," I said. "The man is very big and has trouble walking, but we can help him to the house."

With his wife giving direction, we helped the man to a place by our dining room table. It was not easy, and the weeping had not stopped when he finally squeezed into Claude's captain's chair.

"Oh, you kind, kind folks," the sobbing lady said. "My name is Ginny, and this is John."

She had spoken his name several times as she encouraged him to walk, so we had been introduced, but why were these strangers grieving?

The woman was first to dry her tears. "John and I do a lot of crying," she explained and waited for John to blow his nose. He was still huffing and puffing from the walk to the house, and his stomach did not allow him close to the table.

"Yes, Ginny and I do weep together," he said.

Claude looked helplessly at me, not knowing what to say. And since I didn't know either, I escaped to the kitchen to make coffee.

"We don't drink coffee, dear woman," Ginny said. "You are so kind! Could you possibly make tea?"

"A cup of cold water is enough for me," John said, eyeing the old-fashioned pump in our kitchen. "Does that pump really work?" he asked.

"It gives very good water," I replied, and I pumped a cupful for him.

John nodded a thank you, and his fleshy face lit up. He blew his nose once more and stopped crying. Ginny pumped some water too, and seemed pleased with herself.

"Oooh, ooh, John," she cooed, "Isn't this wonderful? Here we are with these kind and precious folks!"

John agreed and, struggling not to burst into tears, he said,

"Ginny, our dear pastor, rest his soul, would say we were led here."
His voice quavered.

Hastily Ginny interrupted. "Now, now John, don't cry about that
now! But oh, we do miss that dear man, we do." She began to tell
us about their departed pastor and where they were living and how
much the North Country meant to them. We still hadn't learned why
they grieved, or how they had found our home.

Ginny continued her monologue, reporting that for some years
they had vacationed at a resort near Manitowish Waters. "We love
that place," she said. "The folks we rent from are so very special.
This year we planned to see Lake Superior and we have never been
to Little Girl's Point. Well, on the way we saw your signs about
honey, and we just turned into your lane never expecting to find such
dear people as you! You're so kind, serving tea and cake too!"
Ginny's tears welled up once again.

She soon recovered, but her compliments were too frequent.
John had found serenity too, and with it an excellent appetite. He ate
two slices of cake which Ginny fed him, for his girth kept him
beyond reach of his plate. "Ginny is so sweet," he said, and she
smiled lovingly at him.

We still had no idea what had grieved these people, and fearful
of causing more tears, I carefully asked, "Do you have children?"

Yes! Two wonderful boys, and each has two girls and a boy."
Ginny hesitated and looked toward John who seemed not to hear
much of the conversation.

Claude and I began to feel foolish, and finally he said,
"If you need help, Amy, call me. I'll be in my workshop," and the
rascal disappeared.

As he left, Ginny remarked, "Your husband is so sweet and
patient; oh, I love that man!"

It may be a man's privilege to flee, but a woman must sit and
listen. Gradually the story of these two strange people traveling from
Chicago unfolded. Ginny told how many turns they had missed on
the road to Wisconsin. It was this intersection. No, it must have
been that one. But always, kind folks had directed them toward their
goal, the Upper Peninsula North Country. She smiled as her
narration wound down, "It is as if I've always known you, Amy."

John was now perfectly at peace, his arms resting across his vast belly. His red-purplish jowls, still stained from tears, rested on his shirt collar. He slept soundly and snored in a gentle whisper.

Ginny confided that her John was too heavy, that he did not get enough exercise. "We bought the new Cadillac because the steering wheel is adjustable to his size. We so enjoy traveling and making new friends, dear people like you!"

She talked on and on, all about her family, and finally Claude returned, guilt driven, no doubt. As he entered, he shut the door abruptly, awakening John. For just a moment he looked confused, then recovering he said, "I've had my nap in your comfortable chair, Claude. Thank you, thank you, thank you!" Then he turned to his wife and firmly said, "Will we go now to Lake Superior?"

It took all three of us to unglue John from his chair. Ginny tipped it forward while Claude and I pried him loose. We helped him to the deck where all four of us rested and took an extra breath. Still puzzled by the excessive weeping, we led the strange couple to their car.

John drew in his big belly and squeezed himself behind the adjustable wheel. Reaching for the tape recorder he said, "This is a wonderful invention. Ginny and I listen to sermons from our dear pastor, and it is like he is still with us." Again tears began to flow, and Ginny cried along with him.

"Our grandchildren send tapes, too," she sobbed, "and today is John's birthday. We were listening to their greeting as we drove in." Then an inspiration hit her. "Amy and Claude! You are grandparents, you will love to hear their tape, it is so precious."

I did not have the heart to say no, but Claude left mumbling excuses. "It was nice to have met you," the coward said, and retreated to his workshop.

Thirty torturous minutes followed as the children sang and the grandparents sobbed. Then, much comforted, John and Ginny drove down the road through a mist of their falling tears.

At Christmas we received a beautiful card from John and Ginny. "Dear ones," it read, "Our visit with you was the highlight of our summer. We hope to visit next summer. And we have a Christmas tape from grandchildren to share! You will love it, we know, being grandparents too."

Claude said. "How good, Amy, that visitors come to cheer our days." And he headed once more for his workshop.

THE BASKET MAKER

A visitor to the U.P. may admire our trees and beautiful forest, but we who live here know the practical value of wood. Every home has a good woodpile to depend on for heat, and many also have rough-sawn lumber drying in a barn or shack, fine boards for future use.

Our U.P. men like to handle wood with a kind of reverence while making practical items like spoons, shelves, and plain furniture, so we were not surprised when one morning we had an early visitor telling us of his hobby.

"Hey!" he said. "I'm Nick Niemi."

Slamming the door behind him, the stocky man tried to smile. His eyes succeeded, but the fifteen-below-zero temperature this morning had made a mask of his face.

Come in, Nick," my husband Claude said.

"I am in," Nick answered.

"Keep your boots on," I said. "The snow is clean. Would you like a cup of coffee?"

"That's what I came for," Nick responded and reached for the broom to sweep snow from his boots. He walked to our big round table, shivering in his red mackinaw.

He wore an orange wool hat with the flaps pulled down over his ears. His big hands reached eagerly for the mug of steaming coffee, and, helping himself to a piece of cinnamon toast, he dipped it in the cup for his first warm sip.

Waiting while he recovered from the cold, I admired Nick's clothing. Red and orange usually don't match, except when worn by our north woodsmen. Here in the U.P., bright colors bring cheer to our cold days, and this morning Nick was a bright spot in our home. He looked like a sunset on Lake Superior.

Warm and comfortable now, Nick said, "This is a cozy place you got. Glad you came to live here. Heard you come from downstate, eh? Have been lookin' for cedar." He paused.

"Didn't think it to be this cold. Could have frozen to death. I was

42

glad to find you home! Have my car parked at Lake Road and walked all around your property, up to der' belly in snow."

Wondering why Nick was out so early on a cold winter day to look for cedar trees, Claude asked, "You like to walk in the woods, Nick?"

"Yeah. Me, I live in woods too, like you. I was grown up here. My house is someways up hill from Vanderhagen Road, high country. No cedars growing dere."

Nick had a second cup of coffee and more toast, then with a broad smile he told us he was a mason by trade. "Am mostly retired now, but sometimes help people out. You make honey, eh?" he asked Claude.

"No, it is my wife's hobby," Claude answered. He grinned at both of us. My husband will never take responsibility for my apiary, though he handles two tons of honey each summer and fall.

"Give me a quart," Nick said. "I like honey."

"So do I," Claude agreed.

As if not wanting to offend us, Nick told us that we had some beautiful cedar trees on our land. "My hobby is makin' baskets. Learned it from my uncle in Finland. Nobody makes baskets today. When I die, that's the end. Young folks have no patience these days."

He looked at us sadly. "Trees must be right size. Old trees no good. Need straight cedars with about two inches white wood under bark. Dark core don't bend well. Green's too short."

In the wintertime when the woods were open, Nick said, he was out early in the morning to find a new supply for his basket making craft. "Need a half dozen of your cedars now. Can we make a deal?"

"Help yourself, Nick. We don't sell trees. Just take what you need," Claude answered.

Relieved, Nick smiled again, "You good people," he said, and then he told us why basket making is so tricky. He must split a tree trunk, then split each half in three sections. Then he must carefully insert a knife into the soft white layer which lies under the bark and between the core, slicing thin strips one to one-and-a-half inches wide and hopefully four to six feet long, the length needed for making large baskets.

"I make hampers and backpacks," he said. "The shorter strips

43

are for laundry or knitting baskets. My baskets hold up!" he bragged. "Some laundry is still carried in those by daughters who got them from their mothers. Years ago we Finns made lots of useful things from wood: spoons, bowls, brooms, and our own skis. We made spinning wheels and looms for weaving rag rugs, too. Our people help themselves, those old days. Buy nothing."

He confessed he was happy that life would not change for him because we had moved here. "Many times I come to these woods for cedar trees. Nobody lived on this forty."

Well, life changed a little for Nick. Often he came for coffee, and one day I asked him if he would make me a knitting basket in exchange for the trees he selected. It seemed to be a good bargain, and Nick agreed.

As we became better acquainted, I discovered Nick lived with his wife Kate a mile from the road between a mixture of mature hemlocks and maple trees in the deep woods. They had no children. Kate's life revolved completely around her husband and her neat home.

At first I thought they were an unlikely couple. Kate was fiercely possessive of Nick. Though illiterate, she was wise in female affection and proud of her talented husband in a loving way. Her coquettish reactions seemed to hold Nick's interest, and she was a good housekeeper and always neatly dressed.

Kate kept her hair dyed jet black, the color it had been in her younger days. And she used make up lavishly. She may not have had much formal schooling, but she was wise in the ways of women.

Nick and Kate were inseparable, except when he was tramping in the woods, and we became friends. When Nick came for his trees, Kate would wait in the car until I asked her in. When we were not home, she'd let me know in no uncertain terms that we had disappointed Nick. "He wants his coffee!" she told me.

Several times Nick asked Claude to come to his workshop in his basement so he could demonstrate his craft, hoping Claude might want to learn from him. Having asked him to make ten baskets, one for each of our children, we came one day to pay for the order. He charged us a reduced price, and gave me a small basket made of leftovers.

It was amazing to see him at work. His strong, short hands were nimble and quick, bending the water-soaked cedar strips to his will. "With good care, these baskets will last more than twenty years," he said. He proudly praised nature's gift, limiting praise of his own skill.

Intently watching her husband Kate said, "Nick, those baskets make it all the way to Chicago?" Her dark brown eyes were serious and questioning.

"Yeah," he said. "They go far, all over the States."

Nick and Kate became very good neighbors, always present at picnics and socials at Little Girl's Point. One day I was surprised to see Kate play a word game because I knew she didn't know how to read, I watched her win several times. Very attentive, she looked at the cards in front of her, and I soon discovered her secret. The kind persons sitting next to her faked their game and played for Kate. Confident in their trust, she would shout, "Bingo! Nick, I beat you!"

Early one Sunday afternoon, I almost failed Kate. A car stopped at our door. We had not quite finished our dinner. Dressed in their visiting clothes, Nick and Kate walked inside and seated themselves at our table, which I had hastily cleared. As Kate smoked her cigarette, Nick told Claude about our weather. "It's too cold and wet for my garden," he said "Potatoes will rot in the ground. We'll not have tomatoes either."

Kate never talked or discussed her problems; she listened to Nick, nodding and agreeing with what he said, and repeating him from time to time.

"We have been visiting sick friends," she said. Restless, she walked to the window, peering at the dripping trees. "Nick", she said, seeking attention. He did not answer. She called louder,, "Nickolai!"

"Oh, rest awhile, Kate," I said, "the men are visiting."

She focused dark and angry eyes on me and shouted, "Nickolai Niemi! Don't you see? We get nothing to eat here either. It's like at the other place. Why don't we go to Kermit Rice's place?. She will give us a good lunch and coffee. She knows how to treat people."

Nick did not change his tone of voice. Warm and calm, he answered, "Amy gives me coffee. We stay here now, Kate."

"Takes only a minute," I said.

Hurrying to the kitchen, I heard Kate say, "Thought you forgot."

It was on a blustery day in winter that we heard Nick had been taken to the hospital in Duluth. "He had a bad spell," Kate told us on the phone. I had walked that morning down our road to the mailbox and noticed snowshoe tracks leading into the stand of cedar trees. A stump and branches neatly piled to the side told me that Nick had helped himself to a tree, and a deer and some rabbits had found fresh fodder, thanks to his craft.

Missing him that winter, we waited for Nick's return.

One day in late spring, we heard his voice as he walked right into our home. "Come for coffee," he said. Refusing a treat of cinnamon toast, he smiled saying, "The doctors in Duluth told me, no more honey. Must lose weight. Me like an old house, the piping is rusty, all clogged up too. Makin' baskets, fine, but no looking for cedar trees no more. Come only for coffee now, Amy."

He left for good. He made his last basket soon after, and I would like to know who is saving it in his memory. All over the township we recognize Nick's legacy. With care, those baskets will be good for twenty years or longer."

SURROGATE MOTHER

Our people here in the U.P. help each other in practical, sometimes odd, ways. We don't wait for some special need to arise; often we find a way to be a good neighbor. Maybe it's the long winters that make us different, perhaps a bit crazy. Probably the common survival instinct carries over the rest of the year. If that makes us look crazy to the rest of the world, so be it.

One morning my neighbor Olga knocked on our door, unexpected and early. She offered me a large coffee can of worms! Tired looking and yawning, as if she had not had much sleep, she said, "Yech! Here's a can of worms for you, Amy," placing it on the kitchen table. I noticed she held her left hand carefully to her chest. "Shhh," she whispered. "I'm a nursing mother."

"Olga," I said, "Don't fool me. You're at least 60. It's impossible for you to nurse at your age."

Still holding her hand to her breast Olga said, "Do you have coffee ready, Amy?" I poured her a cup and she continued to explain her almost absurd generosity.

"You told me yesterday you and Claude were planning a couple nights at Eel Lake cabin, so I knew you would be going fishing. Well, we have lots of worms, big fat night crawlers we keep in a cooler in the garage. On rainy nights Bill is always happily picking crawlers."

Amazed at my neighbors's good heart, I thanked her several times. Usually Olga's stock answer to thanks for a good deed is "Don't mention it," or, "It's nothing." This time she added, "Amy, I wish I could go fishing with you, but it is impossible. I have to babysit four orphans and nurse them. I hardly slept a wink last night because my babies kept me awake."

Confused, I listened to my friend's complaint. She was obviously too old for babies. Was she going crazy? Hardening of the arteries, maybe?

Pouring more coffee, I wondered if Olga was having heart

trouble. She still clutched her hand to her breast. She is a large person who hates exercise and loves food, but a more loving and giving friend you could not find. What had come over her? Babies to nurse? What babies?

Now relaxing at our dining room table, with one hand still holding her chest, Olga dozed off, muttering, "Thank you, Amy" for the coffee I had poured her.

Finally, I asked, "Do you have a daughter living near who has those babies? While it is fun for us grandmas to babysit, keeping little ones all night at our age is too difficult.

I tried again. "Why did you have to be up all night?"

Bleary eyed, she said wearily, "The mother ran away and left four little ones behind. I couldn't leave them there without help, Amy. Besides, they're so cute!"

Searching for an answer to why her daughter had left her family, I asked, "Where is the father?"

Olga's reply puzzled me even more. "Amy, are you nuts? Who can tell where the father is?" Now she was questioning me!

Beginning to doubt her sanity and wondering about my own, I felt it was best to drop the subject. I poured her another cup of coffee. "Thank you for the worms, Olga," I said, looking gratefully at the can of fat, wriggling crawlers, which I had moved to the floor.

"Those worms started this whole big mess," Olga blurted out. "That's the reason I couldn't sleep all night," Olga continued. "I know when you go to Eel Lake cabin you do a lot of fishing, and you're always anxious to leave, never taking time to pick a good can full of worms. I wanted to help you so you would have fun."

"Poor Bill," Olga sighed, remembering her husbands's miserable, sleepless night with her up every hour nursing babies. She rambled on. "Well, Amy, last night during supper I said to Bill I should surprise you and give you some of the worms. Bill said, Good, but I have to warn you that the worm cooler is behind some junk in the garage. You may find a mouse nest or two back there. I sure did!"

"Olga, you are too good!" I said, meaning it from my heart, "But about your daughter: Why did she run away from her family? And what does that have to do with my worms?"

Olga looked puzzled. "What is the matter with you, Amy? Are you all right? You talk strange! My daughter is home with her children. Why do you ask?"

Shrugging it off, I poured more coffee, not daring to say any more about babysitting.

Suddenly Olga gasped, "Ooh!" she said, clutching her chest with one hand.

"Olga! Are you having heart trouble? Is there anything I can do?"

Shaking her head and carefully holding her hand under her breast, Olga left the table.

I fumbled for something to say. "Are you going home for the next feeding?"

"Oh, no," she replied, "I have my babies right here. Do you want to see them? They're waking up. I can feel them crawling!" Opening her blouse, Olga revealed her four little mice! Bright-eyed, with fine gray hair on pink backs and long tails, they curled together in the shelter of Olga's bra cup. Their heads, surprisingly big, searched for food from an eye dropper neatly clipped to the bra strap!

"They don't need much," Olga explained, "just a drop or two, but I have to keep the milk warm and let them have it every hour. May I feed them here, Amy?"

"Of course," I replied. "I suppose you found them when you were looking for my worms, and their mother ran away." "Now you're making sense, Amy!" Olga said.

MAKIN' WOOD

Fortunately most of our visitors are not as bizarre. Many are helpful people who just come to give us friendly advice. They were genuinely concerned that we from Down Below might not be able to make it through the winter.

One of these men was Hannes Long.

It's "wood makin'" time again. We have now lived for ten years in our beautiful forest, and if all the fire wood we made were stacked along our dirt road, it might reach to our mailbox a half-mile away on the highway.

Actually, we always seem to be makin' wood. Our win-ters, as

we say in the U.P., are long and cold. A big woodpile means that we hope to persevere through the ten months out of the year that we build fires in our stoves. We even have frosty nights in the summer when a "stick or two" are needed for comfort in early morning hours.

Yes, our men all year long bring home a little wood to add to the woodpile. Folks who live here understand our passion for firewood. One of the first visitors to our home in the woods was Hannes Long, a single man. Someone had told me about Hannes, that he was born with a hearing problem, but that in spite of it, he had learned to speak. Hannes spoke in a monotone, often using body gestures to make himself better understood.

You must talk loudly to Hannes, people told me, and because we care about each other here in the U.P., I was informed Hannes is a diabetic and too polite to refuse
sweets, so don't offer them.

That afternoon as Hannes walked slowly toward me from his yellow truck, I noticed that he limped. "Nice house, this," he said. "I hear your kids, your boys, built it so I come to see."

I nodded and asked him in a loud voice to come in and have coffee. As he ate the crackers with a slice of cheese and drank his coffee, Hannes asked, "Heating with wood?" He pointed to our big stove. "You build sauna too? Yah?" Swinging his arms, he declared, "Then you need lots of wood."

"Yes," I said.

Then looking straight at me, he asked the question I was to hear all summer, "You've been makin' wood yet?"

"Not yet, Hannes, it is only July," I said.

He sensed my defensive attitude. "Yeah, yeah" he said and sadly shook his head, leaving me a bit worried.

Meeting my husband at the door, he straightened tall and proudly told Claude, "I already made my wood. Depending on the winter, I have plenty. Might have enough for you too, if you need it."

"Everyone is talking wood," I told Claude. "And it is only the end of July."

Some weeks later Hannes came to see us again. "Makin' wood?" he asked as he came in limping. But this time it was obvious we had been busy. At least two cords of wood were stacked close to the house.

He walked slowly to the pile. "My knee hurts," he said, and he explained why he dragged that bad leg. Years ago a tree fell on him. Working in the woods is a dangerous job.

"You must be careful," he warned. "Those trees are tricky. Some fall and twist where you don't think they will. Others come crashing down in stormy weather. I had a hang-up fall on my leg, a "widow maker, it's called around here."

"What's that?" I asked.

"It's a tree hung up in the top of another that comes down when it's ready to fall. You can't predict it. Woods are dangerous, dan---gerous!" he said.

Most of our men pay for their ambition. Many have lost a finger, some more than one. Don't feel bad, they are proud of it!

The last time we danced at a fiftieth wedding anniversary, Carl, singing with his accordion, stopped the Finnish polka. Surprised, we stood where we were and he called five names: "Ieno, Bill, Elmer, John, Waino; come up here." As the men slowly made their way to Carl, he said, "Hold up your hands, to see how many fingers are missing among you five."

They all laughed, holding up their hands as if they were pledging allegiance. Between the five men four thumbs and three fingers were gone. He counted out "Take a picture, you women," and he held out his own left hand to show us he was playing the accordion bass section with three fingers. "We love our women and the woods. Let's dance again!"

Yes, in the U.P. a man's love for his family can be measured by the woodpiles he makes.

My first woodpile did not look like that made by an expert U.P. woodsman. Some logs were short, others longer, but I told Hannes proudly, "These are downfalls from the last storm. I sawed and split them myself because my husband has been busy finishing the house and his shop."

Hannes shook his head. "Balsam!" he sniffed. "God made balsam to fool people."

"It will burn," I protested.

"Gopher wood," he said slowly. "You 'gofer' more and more. It burns too fast." My proud pile seemed to shrink.

Of course Hannes came in for coffee. We in the U.P. always

have coffee ready, and toast or crackers, too. He sat there, very superior, across from me at the table, trying to tell me all about wood. Cedar is good for kindling. It burns fast and makes a hot fire, but maple is better. "You will need good hard maple, or yellow birch. Don't bother with balsam. Too sticky. It's good for nothing, grabs you every time. You'll learn, Amy, that soft maple is not good either light as a feather when dry. Cherry is not bad, it makes a pretty flame."

I thought, Hannes is nice, and a wise man, too. Admitting my ignorance, I asked him, "How much wood do we need for one winter?"

Again he gave the same answer, "All depends on the kind of winter. You never have too much. Remember you must make good wood, Amy."

August came too fast, and with visitors coming and going, we had no time for making wood. But Claude did build a woodshed of scrap lumber. The week before Labor Day we did make some wood when our children visited and gave us a hand. Also, Claude discovered that LaGrew's saw mill had slabs to be hauled away for free which could be cut into firewood. Most were hemlock, the first saw cut which was to be discarded.

Hannes came again. I knew he was concerned about us. Looking at our woodshed, he seemed pleased and nodded approvingly. Yes, we were on our way. Inspecting what we had stacked, he said, "But that's mostly hemlock, Amy!"

"Yes, Hannes. It looks good, don't you think?" I said it with a smile. At last, I had something to be proud of. Hannes sighed sadly. "That hemlock will not burn by itself. It just lies there smoking. You must have hardwood to burn with hemlock, and even then it does not give much heat." He seemed disappointed with me.

As he followed me into the house for coffee, I asked if he would tell us more about "makin' wood." Encouraged, he explained that we should make several piles, one for a good lasting fire to heat the house with yellow birch, hard maple, or dry elm, which makes lots of ashes but gives a fine fire.

"And then you need polewood," he added.

"Polewood?"

"Yeah." He waved his arms. "Dead maple saplings. You look

53

in woods; many die soon. You pull or push them over. It is good for sauna and your cookstove. Make much and have a second pile of that. Also make a third pile of cedar kindling."

I began to understand. There was much to learn about "makin' wood!"

Finally in October we were finished with the house and could concentrate on firewood. Luckily, many young elm trees had died near our road and they were dry on the stump, the bark peeling away. So on every sunny day of late October my husband and I were busy "makin' wood."

When Hannes again came for coffee and saw what we had in our woodshed, he was all smiles. He brought us apples from his orchard and praised us for "makin' wood," the right wood this time.

Somehow, we came through that first winter which was one of the coldest on record.

It is ten years now since that October, and Gerhard Olson, his son Dean, and our mailman Bertil are helping Claude this afternoon to make wood. Actually, we have plenty of wood for this winter and the next, depending on how severe and long the winter will be. The goal for every man in the U.P. is to have two piles of good firewood, one for this winter and one for next winter. A man's wealth, strength, wisdom, and love for his family all are measured by the size of the woodpile stacked next to his house.

We don't hide our woodpile. We brag about it and show it off, within reason of course. But we talk about how much we have in our basement, and somewhere in the woods a little surplus is hidden so you can help a friend or neighbor.

Oh, your honor depends on it. When we have plenty for ourselves, our men tell each other confidentially, "Last night we cut up a pile of wood for Laura. John, her husband is on the ore boats this fall and doesn't come home until the locks close. Next week we'll cut for Bill; his wife's mother died, you know."

That is how our men talk. We women bake a cake or send a card, but our men heal wounds and ease grief by "makin' wood," lots of it, each man bringing his chain saw and mixture of oil and gas. You don't use someone else's gas; your own gas is always better.

Those wood-makers eat a lot, and there is where we women are important. We cook a big meal of stew or a boiled dinner of beef, cabbage, potatoes, carrots and bagies. Best of all they like an oven roast with potatoes, carrots and onions all in a huge pot. Next there is home made bread with wild raspberry jam, and of course apple pie with two or three scoops of ice cream.

Someone from downstate came by to tell us he thought God made the wood in our beautiful U.P. What does he know? We are makin' our own wood, and makin' wood is an art. Look at our woodpiles. No two are the same. We all do our own thing.

Ernie Smetana stacks it split, perfect in length and size, piling it criss-cross. He stacks it six feet high, row next to row until it makes a nice square pile.

We keep our wood in rounds in an open air shed, the circled pattern making a picture to be proud of.

Bruce Estola builds a sort of igloo with a pointed roof so the rain and melted snow will run off and the inside will stay dry.

The Lepannens build a wall around their house that looks like a fort protecting the home on three sides.

Of course there are shiftless folks who do not care for a neat woodpile at all. They let the logs fall where they may and pick them up as they go. After the snow comes it is a mess!

I have heard downstate folks accusing us of driving too slowly. And they're right. But we take our time because we look at woodpiles. They tell us a lot about the folks who live here in our beautiful U.P.

Anyone who has been through one or two of our winters will understand the hard work which goes into "makin' wood." Our men will tell you that wood will warm you twice: when you make it and when you burn it. But we handle it four times: when you cut it, pile it, store it in your home, and finally bank it in the stove for the long nights.

On your next visit to our beautiful land, take some extra time and admire our country monuments. You can be sure we will give you a warm welcome. Coffee is always ready and our saunas will be hot, and you'll be certain to find someone "makin' wood."

COMING HOME

Had we come to the dense North woods of the U.P. of Michigan only to prove that we could make a place for ourselves in the United States?

I asked myself that question as I looked at the brush piled up in the back of our house. "Were we fools to move here so far north, leaving our children down state?" I said to Claude who was pulling some large branches from the rubble for firewood.

Claude did not answer me involved as he was in the challenge of pioneering. He loved the hard work and freedom. Through the thirty years since we immigrated from Holland he had worked in a tool and die shop. Now after raising our large family we were starting over in the wilderness.

The bulldozer operator who cleared our garden space had told me, "You will never grow anything here Amy; this soil is only good to make pottery. It will take years to built up this hard red clay with top soil."

But I couldn't imagine living here without growing flowers, and I had counted on a vegetable garden to supplement our small pensions. Dismayed, I looked at the ugly heap of gravel and dirt left from the excavating the foundation for our house. In back of the house was a shallow pool with cattails growing where I wanted a green lawn.

"We have to do something," Claude said. "Our property is low and a breeding ground for mosquitos."

"I'd hoped to grow a garden," I answered and wiped a tear hoping he wouldn't notice.

But he did notice. "Are you homesick Amy," You will have a garden, and flowers too," Claude promised."

Where?" I asked, sweeping my hand toward the cattails and a bright blue wild Iris that seemed to grow there for the fun of it. A garden? Flowers? That was a joke.

"Someone told me of Robert and Dick Brace. They do a lot of work to improve property at Little Girls Point." I said.

Claude contacted the brothers who came to look our place over. They suggested that we make a pond and, by digging a small ditch, we could drain our property.

"We'll spread the dirt that we remove from that pond and you'll have your garden, Amy" Robert said.

"We'll have to take some of your favored trees," Dick added, pointing to a large blue spruce.

I knew some sacrifices were to be made, but I asked him to save the crooked old hemlock near where they were digging the pond.

"That tree? Its a bad one!" Dick snorted like a true woodsman.

"But it will look pretty with snow piling on its branches." I protested. Dick shook his head.

"We'll leave it just for you, Amy."

"Thanks!" I said, "and please leave that big rock, the one near the tractor."

Dick winked at Robert. "Just for you, Amy." The brothers liked to tease a city woman.

But which trees were to be saved? All were special to me. I told Claude, "You may take every tree in the forty except the ones growing near our home."

Growing a garden was not easy, even with the soil removed from the pond. I planted our first potatoes in the molding old hay bales. The carrots grew fat and short. My chrysanthemums, brought from our house down state, froze before they flowered. My helpful neighbor, Libby Brace, gave me shoots from her lilacs and an old fashioned red rose bush.

Another lady, learning of my love for flowers, told me, "Come over and help yourself to some of my perennials, Amy." Mrs. Roman's flower garden was a show place.

I bought six old hens from a friend on Lake Road for one dollar each. And then got my first goat, Narna.

Amazed, our neighbors began to name our place, "The farm, the home of milk and honey." Narna gave us gallons of milk, and I learned how to make the soft squeaky cheese the Finns like so well.

Goat's milk is not only nutritious but naturally homogenized. Some people who don't tolerate cow's milk will digest goat's milk better because of its smaller fat cells. It tastes like cows milk when refrigerated immediately after milking. In our climate, goat's milk is best in winter, when I place the fresh milk in a snow pile to cool.

All winter long Narna is kept warm lying in her stall on a bed of hay that spills from her crib. She wets her bed regularly lying in it, composting a fine fertilizer for my garden. Inch by inch Narna has helped me build fertile soil on the hard clay for a good garden. Unfortunately one day she died of pneumonia.

In return for the help our friendly neighbors gave us, Claude gave of his talents. Often the area churches needed an organist and he substituted many times that first year at Immanuel Lutheran, Little Girls Point, or at St. John's Lutheran where he played on a big old pump organ.

We had become part of the community, although isolated in the woods. And yet the same question kept returning "Was this to be my home?"

"Aren't you lonely?" visitors and tourists who stopped by would ask. The quiet of a forest can be intimidating to those who are used to noise. Some days we don't see a car or hear a human voice but that of our own.

"No," I tell the hurrying tourists, "We aren't lonely; we hear the many voices of the forest."

It was late spring. Orange swamp lilies bloomed brightly, the trilliums had turned to a muted pink, and purple lupines completed the wildflower show. With beauty and splendor the Northwoods welcomed Claude and me to our retirement home in Michigan's Upper Peninsula.

Why then, surrounded by all that beauty, did a strange restlessness steal over me? Something, or someone, seemed missing. The feeling would not go away.

Each day I wandered the forest surrounding our new home, perhaps thinking I might find an answer to my restlessness in the reminders left behind by those who had once lived near by. Small trails led to old shacks tucked back in the brush and spring blossoms. Once men came to those shacks; there they lived, hunted, and died. The shabby outhouses belonging to each shack had been ravaged by generations of porcupines that chewed the wood for traces of salt left by sweating rumps.

From a tall hemlock one of the quilled bandits looked down at me. The hollow hemlock, I perceived, was his home; the tree crown his breakfast table. He seemed content, but I was not.

Then one midsummer day when the berries were ripe, I took my pail and walked up our road alone. I came upon an overgrown drive I hadn't explored. A faded sign told me this was the Laura Fredrickson Homestead. People from Little Girl's Point had told me about Laura Fredrickson, the only other woman ever to live along our forest road.

Hesitantly, I approached a vacant house built of large pine logs. Unlike the hunting shacks, this house was in fine shape. Near the house stood the ruins of an ancient barn. Lush raspberries grew on its north side, the canes bowed by the weight of ripe berries. I picked my bucket full, thanking the dead woman who planted them.

Now tired and hot, I rested on Laura's back steps and sampled her berries. A deep longing swept over me. If only Laura could open the door and call, "Amy, coffee's ready!"

Rising stiffly, I peered through a dusty window at Laura's kitchen. Had her days grown lonely on this quiet road too? Had she sometimes wondered why she moved to the woods? Had she too felt that something or someone was missing?

I looked again toward the barn. A poplar sapling reached up from the rubble. Sheltered between decaying boards, the sapling seemed in a hurry to mature, to retake the terrain from the invader. Wild pink sweet peas sprawled over the crumbling stone foundation as though bent on hiding man's short-lived labor. Behind the barn stood a rusting, cast-iron pump, its use long spent. And beyond the pump were a row of maturing spruce and fir, a fine windbreak. At least the homesteaders had left behind something enduring!

Sweet williams had seeded themselves generously to the south of Laura's house, and as I walked among them, I again wondered if she had known my loneliness, my hunger for woman talk?

I heard myself say, "You have such a friendly place, Laura! How long since you lived here?"

I found Laura's garden. Wispy asparagus still grew, and in a corner, clumps of rhubarb struggled to survive. How long does it take to erase a woman's garden? Many, many years.

Laura felt close, still living in things she had planted. Indeed she was close, talking with me in her garden! Comfort and belonging flowed over me.

I chatted with Laura as I walked slowly home. I told her how sweet her berries were. Might I transplant some of her rhubarb? I promised to return with manure for her rhubarb, so once again the stalks would grow red and strong. I asked if I could take some sweet williams for the garden at my new home.

I knew Laura would understand. She had lived many years in the woods, she had made her world more beautiful, and now I would borrow some of her beauty. It was only right that I should.

Quickly and joyously the years passed. Our home in the woods became my sanctuary. Experimenting with hardy plants, I improved our garden, each year adding new varieties of flowers, vegetables, trees, and shrubs. Then one summer Sunday afternoon, two women came to our door.

The taller one spoke first. "Can you tell us where we can find the old Fredrickson place?" She nodded toward the smaller woman at her side, "We are looking for her mother's old homestead."

The smaller woman looked up. She carried a gray box. "Do you have any idea if the house is still standing? I hope it's not that shack across the road!"

"No," I laughed, "That's just a hunting cabin. Please, won't you come in?"

The smaller woman placed the gray box gently on the counter near the sink. "We've been driving back roads all afternoon!" she sighed. "I'm Irma, Laura Fredickson's daughter."

As I made coffee, Irma told how much her mother had loved her long years in the U.P. But after Mr. Fredrickson died, she moved to New York. "You're sure her home is still there?" she asked, glancing toward the gray box.

"Oh, yes," I assured her, "it's a fine log house; second forty up the road. The people who now own the property have kept it up well but they found the U.P. too remote and retired to Arizona."

"Your mother's home is such a friendly place," I added. "I visit there often. It has become special to me. The sweet williams in our garden came from your mother's yard." Again Irma's eyes sought the gray box.

"Mother so loved the woods," she said softly. "All through the years in New York, she longed for her home here." Then she added, "Do you actually live here in the winter?"

I laughed. "We enjoy the seasons! I would find it hard to live in New York! We no longer feel at home in the city."

"Mother was so old when she died," Irma said. "Ninety three." She sat silently, then asked, "May I see your garden?"

"Of course!" I replied. The taller woman and I watched Irma move among the flowers, her small figure bending to smell a rose. For just a moment, I saw Laura picking a deep red sweet william!

The taller woman spoke in a low voice, "This is all new to Irma, she knows only the city. She loved her mother so dearly. This will help with her grieving."

The women took snapshots of our home and garden, then thanked me and prepared to leave. We stepped inside briefly, and Irma picked up the gray box reverently. "I've come to bring Mother home," she said. "These are her ashes."

RESTORATION

The shacks dotting our woods are temporary shelters for men who for one or two weeks out of a year come to hunt, pretending to be providers as in days past, putting meat on the family table.

But a few of the shacks also serve as a retreat for men who would escape a demanding job in town. Such as was the man who owned a camp across the road from our home. He was a frequent visitor.

"Life is very lonely for me now," Joe Spanoli said. Joe was our only neighbor. He owned a run-down hunting camp across Partridge Road from our home in the U.P. woods. Joe found me in the yard. He held his left arm behind his back, and with his right he gave me a big hug then kissed my hand like Italians do and said, "I brought you something for coffee, Amy."

"I'll make a fresh pot, Joe," I said, and I hurried ahead of him to the house, leaving the door open. Slowly, very slowly, he followed, breathing heavily and pausing to rest before climbing the steps to our porch. Then walking to the table, he presented his gift. "Here, Amy, this is good stuff, but you must drink it in your coffee." He placed a bottle of homemade wine in front of me.

"There aren't many bottles with good screw tops," Joe said. "Will you save it for me?"

Assuming that he had not brought baked goods to go with the coffee, I found a coffee cake I had made that morning and set it in front of Joe. He had opened the bottle and poured his "good stuff" in my cup, nearly filling it. "I don't know what kind of wine this is. My son makes it," Joe explained. He eyed the coffee cake, and after he'd eaten three slices, I said he could take the rest home.

Shaking his head sadly, he said, "Home is not home anymore since my Viola died. I got hit twice, Amy. My little dog Lady died two weeks after Viola. I've nothing to live for anymore. That's why I come here to the woods to putter away part of day in my little cabin."

"You don't taste the wine, Amy!" he said. "You must try my

good stuff."

I took a swallow of the coffee-wine mixture. I'd added lots of sugar, and it wasn't bad. Joe began to feel better after his second cup of coffee, and after eating more coffee cake, there wasn't much to take home.

For a long time I listened as Joe told about Viola, what a beautiful girl she had been, always, always happy. "She was everything to me, a good dancer, a good cook." He told how she would joke and fool him sometimes. "The men who came hunting were jealous of me." Smiling at the memory of his wife, Joe wiped away tears.

"And my little snauzer Lady, she was my second best friend, Amy. By St. Peter! That dog was so smart, me and my Viola, we had to spell out words or she'd know what we were talking about."

It had been almost noon when Joe came, and at one-thirty he was still talking about his Viola and Lady. Claude came in to see when I'd have lunch ready, and when I invited Joe to have a bowl of soup with us, he declined. "No, no. Mercy me! Is it that late, Amy?' He stood up quickly, wiping his eyes with the back of his hand. Swaying a little, he made it to the door. "Thank you, folks," he said. "Take care now."

"What's in that vinegar bottle?" Claude asked.

"It's not vinegar but 'good stuff', a wine Joe brought me. You must mix it in your coffee, he told me."

I stood up to warm Claude a bowl of soup and make us a sandwich, but the kitchen seemed to turn, with the floor rising. Or was I swinging? It was safer to sit on the floor. I looked at Claude and he was moving oddly too. I heard him ask, "Amy, are you sick?" He seemed to be far away.

"No!" I said. "only a little drunk, I think. I was trying to be nice to Joe when he put lots of his good wine in my coffee. I must have been drinking it on my empty stomach. Oh, I feel horrible!"

"You've been too polite, too friendly," Claude said, and he took the bottle from the table to the sink.

"No, don't throw it in the sink " I protested. "I'll find a use for it. Just please bring me a bowl of soup and I'll be fine."

Three days later when stewing a rabbit Claude had shot in our swamp, I detected a very strong cedar odor. Of course! Fresh green

63

cedar was the rabbit's food supply. I remembered Joe Spanoli's wine. Fine cooks in fancy restaurants use cooking wine to marinate meat. Since this was a dry wine, it should work fine. I poured all of Joe's "good stuff" on that tough rabbit. The alcohol would boil off, and Claude would never know.

Personally, I don't care at all for wild meat, but Claude likes it. At dinner time he took a forkful of rabbit. "Mmmm! Different," he said. His second bite brought more comment. "Is this the rabbit? I can't believe it!"

My husband will eat almost anything. He has eaten porcupine, raccoon, beaver, muskrat, bear and fish of all kinds. "Yes, that's the rabbit you shot last week," I answered.

Claude took another bite, then he asked, "Amy, why is this rabbit so sour? What did you put on it? It doesn't taste like rabbit."

I had to confess, "The rest of Joe Spanoli's wine." I've heard that in fancy restaurants they cook with wine."

"Don't you ever accept wine from him again!" Claude warned as he disposed of the rabbit.

Thereafter, at regular intervals Joe came to our home, always carrying another bottle of wine behind his back. I'd pour enough to taste, and to be polite to Joe. He would talk about his little wife Viola and Lady, his snauzer dog.

Losing both of his loved ones in two weeks was more than Joe and his heart could bear. One morning he came to tell me he'd been getting out of breath lately. He'd gone to a doctor who advised him to see a specialist in Marshfield and have heart surgery. "My pump needs repair," he said. "So good-bye, Amy. I may see you again, or I may not!"

It was not very long, perhaps a month, before Joe visited, again, with his surprise behind his back. "We must celebrate, Amy," he said smiling. "Yes, they had me in for repair there at Marshfield, putting in all new tubing. Now I can work hard in camp, cutting wood for deer season. It's easy for me to breathe now."

"We must not overdo the celebration," I warned.

"No, just one toast for you, one for Claude and one for my new heart," Joe proposed.

"No, we'll combine it all in one long toast," I replied. This is wonderful news, Joe!" I wished him good luck, a long life, and much happiness.

Several months passed before Joe visited again. This time he did not come with a bottle behind his back. Now his left arm held a very nice lady.

"Come meet my new wife, Nelda," he said, and he graciously led her into our home. "I've been telling Nelda about your home. Today I said we must go see Amy and Claude living in the woods near my camp. Nelda likes to hunt and likes to live in my cabin."

They were so much in love. Nelda assured me she liked outdoor living and had camped all over the U.S. Then she added, "We will fix that cabin and come often to keep you from being so lonely, you poor folks. Now you must come visit us. You'll never be alone now."

Joe had his arm wrapped around her shoulder and she kept her hand on his knee, as if to prevent him from leaving. Constantly talking, she assured me how lucky we were to be their neighbors.

We were happy for Joe, but the thought of having close neighbors was appalling. We weren't in need of neighbors; we enjoyed being the only people living on North Partridge Road.

When Nelda and Joe came to fix up their cabin, our half- mile walk to the mailbox took us past their place, always bringing an invitation. Every morning Nelda would ask if I would come in for coffee. When I declined she would say, "Maybe you would enjoy a glass of dandelion wine, Amy?" "Not at nine in the morning," I would politely reply.

When I tried to sneak through the woods trail to the mailbox, Nelda seemed to know. She would be waiting for me at the end of the road.

Joe kept busy, painting the kitchen ceiling and walls and putting fancy trim on the windows. We did not see much of him. When the little cabin was almost fixed up inside, Claude and I were invited to celebrate Joe's accomplishments. "I've kept to myself because my Nelda told me I should have new teeth," Joe said. "The dentist has been grinding and chiseling and he capped them. How do I look?" Joe flashed a beautiful smile at me. "From now on I always smile to my Nelda, hey girl? Cost me too much money. This is my thousand dollar smile, Amy. But my wife's happy, aren't you, Nelda?"

"He's like a young man again," she laughed. "What's money good for? Now you're my handsome man, Joe!"

"We make a toast to cabin and to my new teeth," Joe said.

In the U.P. June brings multiplying bugs, especially black flies, that drive everyone from the woods. Then, even the walk to the mailbox can be unbearable because the bloodthirsty gnats bite just above the socks and collars, crawling in the eyes, ears and hair. Then we must take our truck instead of enjoying the mile-long walk. Even in the cab we fight the bugs. Fortunately, in two weeks the worst of the black fly ordeal is over. We can cope with the other insect hordes: mosquitoes, deer flies, horseflies and the stinging fishflies of Lake Superior.

During the black fly invasion Joe and Nelda stayed in town, but they returned to their cabin to celebrate the Fourth of July, bringing firecrackers and sparklers.

This time Joe came alone to visit us. Nelda was having fun with her grandchildren who had come to camp. Proudly he told us of his latest improvement. "Folks, I want you to know that I'm almost a new man now." Then pausing, he counted on his fingers. "First I had a new heart, then a new wife and after that new teeth. That makes three." He came closer to let me look in his kind brown eyes. "I even have new eyes! Cataracts come out, new lens put in. Good as new."

"I'll put nice siding on cabin over tarpaper, next fall maybe. I've had trouble with hernia, but that's fixed too. Doctor tells me not to lift anything for three months." Stretching as if he wanted me to see for myself the new man he was, he announced, "Yes, am all new, restored and fixed up. Now you come over to my camp for a glass of lemonade. We'll celebrate. Yea, Lemonade! I new man now. Doctor told me to drink lots of lemonade. Good stuff, full of vitamins." Glancing at Claude, I told Joe we'd be there in a few minutes.

At Joe's camp we toasted his good fortune with lemonade, but sipping my tall glass of it was not quite the same. Somehow I missed that awful other "good stuff." Even the sugar cookies Nelda had baked were lemon flavored.

"Now Joe is making siding for the camp," Nelda said. "We're thinking of dark brown with yellow trim for the windows."

"But first we need new roof," Joe said. "Nelda's going to carry up shingles. I nail them down. Me and my Nelda will work hard all next week. I feel very good," he said beaming at his Nelda.

Joe looked very handsome. What was so different about him today? Then I knew. His thick gray hair was now a shiny black! Nelda, you've performed a miracle with this man, I thought.

The following week a truck from the lumber company in town unloaded new shingles, some slats, and a big pail of roofing cement at Joe's cabin. He and Nelda followed right behind. And like Joe had said, Nelda climbed the ladder to the roof supplying him with small piles of shingles.

At times I heard Joe singing, pounding in a steady rhythm. Happy for my new neighbors, I began to feel guilty, having for a time begrudged them the joy of sharing my woods. Fortunately there will be days when they'll be living in town, and all will be just like it was before.

About four o'clock the pounding stopped. He's taking a break, I thought. Nelda had told me she would drive to town for yellow paint for window trim while Joe was working on the roof. "I must keep an eye on that young man!" she had said.

Returning with the paint, Nelda found it oddly still around the cabin. Then she found Joe, face down on the ground, the hammer still clutched in his hand. He'd fallen off the roof.

The restoration of Joe's cabin went unfinished and once again only Claude and I live on Partridge Road. But I miss Joe and Nelda.

OUR SARAH CIRCLE

I must not give the impression that living in the forest thirteen miles north of Ironwood means that we are isolated from the larger community in town.

Because of Claude's organ playing we soon made many friends, people who come to visit us. We visit them too. Both of us having different interests joined several clubs. Claude has his monthly meetings of the Range Wood Carvers Club where he learns ways to enrich his talents to create works of art. I belong to the Pewabic Pens. Besides being involved in church activities we also go to concerts at the restored old theater in Ironwood. Occasionally we see a play at "Theater North".

But the friendship that I find very especially rewarding is that with my Finnish neighbors in North Ironwood,the ladies who attend St. Johns Church on Airport Road.

Let me tell you of the fun and friendship I share with the women of the Sarah Circle at one of their Christmas parties.

I placed the last ornament, a pretty white angel, on the top of our tall Christmas tree then buried my face in some of its green branches and crushed a small twig between my fingers and inhaled the pungent smell. With that, the preparation for our annual Sarah Circle Christmas party was finished.

A potluck luncheon was planned for our little group at noon, but I knew some of my friends would come early to offer their help.

First to arrive were Laura, Sayma, and Eleanor. I heard them on the steps brushing the snow from their boots with the broom provided for that purpose. We always need that broom. It's a U.P. ritual comparable to Arabian foot washing, because we can have snow nine months of the year here in Lake Superior land.

It did not take long before all the ladies had lined up their boots on the stone entrance of our back door. In the U.P. we don't use our front doors for our friends. Front doors are for funerals and such. Also, during winter months, the front door is tightly closed to keep cold drafts from entering.

Each lady brought a pair of knitted slippers to keep her feet warm. Soon twenty ladies sat visiting comfortably in our living room. All were dressed up for the party, with jewelry and beads to match the gaily decorated tree, and all were in their sixties or seventies or not telling!

Dressed in a bright red suit with gold jewelry, Sylvia Neimi smiling happily hugged everyone. Complimenting her taste I said, "Red is a very good color for you, Sylvia. You look gorgeous."

"Thank you!" she beamed. "Red is my favorite color, though most Finnish women prefer blue." Then suddenly giggling Sylvia said, "Ladies, do you know something is very wrong here?" All the ladies turned to Sylvia in surprise. What could it be?

"Have you noticed we're all Finn? At least we all have Finnish names. But here is poor Amy, and she is Dutch!"

"How can we change that?" Sayma Walkonen asked. Twenty ladies of the Sarah Circle, looking worried at me, seriously tried to find a solution.

"She married a Dutchman, too, poor thing," Eleanor added. "I at least married a Finn and got a Finnish name."

"Please, isn't it enough to be your friend," I begged. "I'm too old to get a divorce."

"No, no," Sylvia declared, "it's not that difficult. We can do something. We can make Claude a Finn too by simply adding <u>nen</u> to Amy's last name. From now on you will not be Van Ooyen but <u>Claude and Amy Van Ooyennen.</u> That sounds right!" Sylvia's proposal met with loud applause, and I proudly accepted the challenge of my new nationality.

So we celebrated with a fine Christmas luncheon, and as always there was too much good food. The table groaned with a great variety of Finnish Christmas delicacies made from recipes that had been carried over for generations from mother to daughter. There were fish soups and salads, rice puddings with boysenberry sauce, Christmas <u>stoller</u>, and soft squeaky cheese, cardimon bread, and fried spiced hardtack. Later in the afternoon Pastor Maki of St. John's Church would come with his family, and there was plenty for them too. After our meal we sang the old Christmas carols. Then Marion Saari, a very good reader, recited a poem from an old magazine about Christmas 75 years ago. We could almost hear the sleigh bells ringing!

Years ago Eleanor Aho's mother had written many interesting stories of early holidays. Although they have never been published, Eleanor honors her by reading her original tales at Christmas. We love them too.

Because today was a party, we kept our business meeting short and tabled requests from church headquarters for money, saying, "It is better to save it. We may need it for our own. Why should we give our offering to folks we don't know?"

Our Bible study, outlined in a monthly publication, took the usual 20 minutes. This lesson was easy to understand by us women who live near Lake Superior. The story was about Jesus calming the storm on Lake Galilee. By setting the miracle at the place where we now live, we imagined Jesus sleeping peacefully in Waino Walkonen's boat on Lake Superior and we turned the Lord's fishermen disciples into men who live at Little Girl's Point.

It was Waino who shouts against the howling wind and water, "You sleep now? We ready to drown! Hey, my boat's sinkin'!" Jesus quietly speaks and the waters become calm.

Yes, we women have experienced many a storm in our lives and most were calmed by our Lord's loving care.

Then it was time for fun and games, and Bertha told us to place a sheet of paper on our head and draw a Christmas tree on it. Our arms ached from trying. Saime Walkonen won because she drew a star that landed right on top of the tree she had scribbled.

The event we were really looking forward to was the opening of cards and presents from our "Secret Prayer Pal" of the year. In the U.P. everybody knows almost everyone and everything, but the identity of our "Prayer Pal" is the most carefully guarded secret among us women in this area.

Last year my friend Laura drew my name at the Christmas party and she kept me guessing all year long. Almost monthly I received very religious cards. They came also for my birthday, anniversary and all the holidays! Even on St. Urho's Day, my Secret Pal wrote a verse under the ugly green grasshopper. (St. Urho is a mythical Finnish saint who drove all the grasshoppers out of Finland, suspiciously like St. Patrick did with the snakes of Ireland). For St. Valentine's Day too my card was very serious! Laura had me fooled because she likes to be funny and loves a joke. I never expected her as my Secret Pal.

Sylvia Neimi is good at fooling us too, but last year Mayme Lepponen tricked her by sending cards picturing cats. She pasted a cute kitten over St. Urho's grasshopper. For her birthday, Easter, and all holidays Sylvia received cat cards; tom cats, calico females, and fluffy kittens. Sylvia thought the cards came from Selda Talo who is a fanatic cat lover. When Sylvia opened her Christmas card and found another cat wishing her happy holidays, she couldn't believe it was from Mayme Leppanen who hates cats!

When we were ready for dessert Pastor Maki and his family arrived. Having promised to make a cake, I said, "We are now going to eat Dirt Cake."

Several ladies pulled up their noses and agreed with Mildred Kantalla. "We aren't eating dirt, Amy," she protested.

Pointing to the center piece on the table, a bright red poinsettia in a decorated flower pot, I said, "But this is good dirt, Mildred, why don't you test it?

Carefully taking a pinch between her thumb and forefinger, Mildred smelled it then tasted it. "Not bad, Amy! That's good North Ironwood dirt, full of minerals and iron," and she held out her plate for more.

"No," I said, "The center piece is for the person who has a birthday or anniversary nearest to today. I have another pot of the same good dirt in the kitchen for all of you."

"Bill and I have our fortieth anniversary tomorrow!" Mildred said, surprised that she was the winner and smacking her lips in anticipation of more dirt cake.

Congratulating Mildred and applauding her long marriage, it was fun to see her claim a pot full of "dirt" under a plastic poinsettia to take home to her Bill who had farmed all his life in the U.P..

"Amy, don't forget and give that recipe to my wife," pastor Maki said as he ate his portion of the novel chocolate cake. "But you should have put a little worm in it!"

"You make me sick, pastor." Mildred protested, probing the "dirt" in the flower pot with her finger, wondering if I had tricked her.

When it was time to go home the ladies left reluctantly. We

old ladies sure had fun and knew that during January and February there would be no meeting, for temperatures often reach 25 below with snow piling up over 200 inches!

But luckily we could expect a January thaw, and that is when Sayma Walkonnen organizes a special event at her place. It's "The Sarah Circle Grandmothers' Ski Marathon."

Her husband Waino grooms ski trails through the woods and does special things to make the day an adventure for us. We never know where the trails will lead. He places crazy signs in the snow, but some are in Finnish, others in Latin.

"Oh, easy readin' for you too, Amy," he says. "Say all letters and you right. In Finn you do. No silent letters, hey?"

So we start at the sign that says "Alpha and Omega." And we know that Waino has fooled us when we come to a sign that says "Sarah Circle" because we have been going around and around in circles through his woods.

When finally we arrive at Sayma's home a potluck lunch is always waiting and there's plenty of reason to cheer ourselves. Sisu! to us and the Sarahs!" We shout. We have won another day of winter!

Yes, Sayma assured us, she would call us on a nice January day and everything was ready for the annual race.

When the women were gone, our home seemed to be deserted. I opened my gaily wrapped present left on the table by my Prayer Pal. The box held two pot holders and a bright blue knitted dishcloth, all made especially for me, Amy Van Ooyennen. With it was a card wishing me and my family happy holidays. It was a gift from the one Sarah we had laid to rest that year.

DIRT CAKE

1 LARGE PACKAGE OREO COOKIES, CRUSHED. (THE WHITE FILLING MAKES IT LOOK LIKE VERMICULITE.)

1 PACKAGE CREAM CHEESE

1/2 CUP POWDERED SUGAR

1 PACKAGE INSTANT VANILLA PUDDING

1 CUP MILK

Make the pudding and mix it with the cream cheese, then fold in a 12 oz. package of Dream Whip.

Use the plastic Dream Whip cover to seal the hole in the bottom of a seven-inch flowerpot (red clay or plastic). Place first a layer of crushed Oreo cookies, then the cream mixture. Alternate layers, but have a layer of Oreo crumbs on the top.

Decorate with a seasonal flower or geranium. Cool and refrigerate. Serve with a scoop or a new garden trowel. (A rubber worm is optional, depending on what your guests may appreciate!)

Note by Amy: This recipe makes a large amount of heavy, rich dirt cake....yummy for the tummy. I used two seven-inch pots and almost filled both. I gave one for a door prize.

Anyway, thats how we spent our winters in the U.P. having fun.

MARY YOUNG'S GIFT

Our quiet dirt road stretched out ahead of me, ending abruptly near a tall balsam tree a quarter of a mile past our home where the county had cleared a space for the snowplow to turn. Beyond our driveway, the road narrows into a muddy two-track trail. Only hunters drive beyond us in the fall, their heavy pickups carrying them to their camps or to make winter wood.

Returning from a trip to Lake Superior one fine spring day, I saw several vehicles parked on our road. Since this was so unusual, I was sure something must be desperately wrong. I saw my husband Claude motioning for two trucks to stop as he was trying to direct the driver of an older car into our driveway. All that was visible above the car's dashboard was a little red hat. Whoever was behind that wheel obviously had not had much driving experience.

I recognized the man in one truck. He was smoking a big cigar, and he owned a cabin near us in the woods. His nickname was "Stoogie," but we called him the "Polish Prince", which is the name of the hunting camp he built. Patiently waiting, he seemed to enjoy the activity and Claude's frustration. The driver of the truck behind him however had little sympathy. Shouting obscenities, he added spice but not much support to the person desperately trying to maneuver her old car as she attempted to back up to our home. She tried over and over again, making too short a turn and nearly colliding with a maple tree beside Claude's workshop.

"Claude, why don't you help drive the car to the house?" I suggested.

"She won't let me. She's stubborn like a mule," he said, perspiring and exhausted on that warm Sunday afternoon. "Will you tell her? Please, Amy!"

Parking our truck on the road, I found Mary Young behind the wheel. Even when sitting on two pillows, she could barely see above the dashboard, and her feet hardly touched the floor of her large Chevrolet.

"Mary, what a nice surprise!" I told her. "Come with me to our home. Welcome to our place in the woods."

Vibrant and happily making excuses, she popped from the seat and told me. "I'm so sorry, but I wanted to do this myself."

"Claude will drive your car to our home. You don't have to back up, our drive circles around the evergreens."

"I was practicing," she answered, as if reluctant to give in.

Dressed in a black pantsuit and red blouse, a red hat matching her red lipstick, the old lady was cute, feisty as ever, and not the least embarrassed about her defeat.

"I almost made it," she said. "This was good practice for me. I got my new drivers license last week and I was going to surprise you. I brought you a present, too."

Mary talked so fast there was no way to stop her. "I've not learned to go in reverse yet," she said. "I was afraid I'd back into gravestones. I've been driving around and around, always going forward when practicing in the cemetery. Every evening this summer I do it. It's so convenient and close to my home. At least I could not kill anyone there, and there's not much traffic at all."

She laughed a little and told me the examining officer was very pleased with her performance. "Take it slow, Mary," he had said. "And stay on the back roads."

"I wanted to do this myself," she told me again. "With Deany gone and Gladys too, it is important to be independent, and now I will travel and see the world."

"Mary, not by driving your car!" I asked astonished at her determination.

"No, the officer told me not to drive on the highway, but I will go on bus tours. And I have presents for you before I go see the country. These are some things you must need when your children visit."

"Mary, come and see our home," I invited.

"No, first things first. Claude why don't you open the trunk of my car?" She fumbled with the keys. "You take those, take all that is in there to the house. Take all that stuff!" she commanded.

As Claude carried the boxes inside, Mary followed. "There are some old dishes here and I want you to have them all." Once inside our home she seemed to be pleased. "Yes," she said. "I was right.

You will do a lot of entertaining here. It's a beautiful home, just like you see in magazines."

"No, Mary. It is home to us, but not an expensive place. Please sit down, you are so welcome."

Mary was too excited. Chattering to herself, she began to open the boxes and now it was my turn to be excited. She unwrapped a place setting of very expensive china. "This is complete for twelve," she explained,. "with bowls and serving dishes too ." And there was more: a silver tea and coffee server, a dozen cut lead crystal dishes in various shapes, and sterling silver flatware for eight.

Mary talked and I was speechless. "You have a nice house and now you have what you need," she said, very pleased with herself. "Deany and I never had much. But all my relatives are gone now, and I have no use for these things anymore. You have many children, and I have much money. Gladys left everything to me. She was married to a rich man."

I listened to Mary telling me her family story how one niece had married a wealthy man much older than herself. She did not want to leave her mother, so she lived next door to her husband with her invalid mother and took care of both homes. When her husband died, the mother did not live very long, and soon the niece was gone too. "So I got all the money, and you have all the dishes. Let's have a tea party now. I brought sweet rolls too!"

"Would you like to use the nice dishes, Mary?" I asked.

"No," she said. "A mug is good enough for me. Deany and I were never fancy."

Mary chattered again to herself, babbling about the family and all who were so dear to her. We answered "Yes, Mary," over and over again and told her she should visit us often.

Claude soon fled to his workshop, and as Mary and I drank our tea from plain mugs, she shyly asked about the cabin at Eel Lake. "Do you have a problem with the Forest Service, too?" she asked.

"No," I replied, "we have everything in good repair. Come over and see it soon. Since you have the key, you can make yourself a cup of tea if we are not at the lake."

" Yes, I will," she said. " Are my looneys still near the rock?"

"Yes, they have one baby and are waiting for you, Mary."

"What are you paying for the lease now?" she asked.

"One hundred sixty dollars a year," I told her.

She nearly jumped from her chair. Rolling her eyes she began to scold the government. "Robbery! Robbery! We used to pay only twenty five-dollars. Then was up to forty! You will not sell it?" she asked anxiously.

"No, Mary, we will not, never. We love your cabin."

"It was Deany's cabin," she said quietly.

"He must have had a real love for nature to preserve that beautiful spot and leave the white birch growing right up to the cabin door," I said, praising his choice.

"He did, but I was the one who told him about the cabin. I was working for the Forest Service at that time, and I knew which lots were being leased. We bought a stand of mature cedar in the swamp down the hill, and Deany used them to build our cabin with his own hands. He carried every log on his back over two hills. It took him four years before the cabin was finished, but he was a strong man, Deany was!"

She shook her head. "I have to go home now, but I will return soon and bring a friend. Next week I'll travel to the East Coast, to Boston and Washington. I'll call you when I am safely back from my adventure."

I asked her if Claude should drive the car out to the road for her, but she declined. "I must do it myself."

Hugging me she said, "I was going to put you in my will, but I see now you don't need it. You and Claude are rich! I love you, and will come often."

Mary would usually visit us two times during the summer, early in the spring, and later in fall, and we always used the fine china for a tea party. Sometimes she brought a friend, on other Sunday afternoons she'd come by herself.

We were relieved to see her drive a new car, much smaller and easier to handle. Although Mary still had to sit on a pillow. she said. "I don't need forty acres to turn around now. This car has power steering."

At Christmas time, when her car was stored for the winter, I brought Mary to our home to admire our Christmas tree which reached up to the high cathedral ceiling of our living room. A child could not look with more wonder at the bright lighted balsam we had cut from our property.

Every year we received a Christmas greeting from Mary with a one-hundred-dollar check. To explain her generosity she wrote, "to help you pay for the lease of my cabin." Gradually she was repaying us what we had paid her for her cabin.

On her last visit late in August Mary was less happy and vibrant and very quiet. "I do not have much appetite but may I have tea in my little cups, please?" she asked. She sat comfortably in a chair and was in no hurry to leave for home.

"Mary, would you like to have lunch here?" I asked. "Claude is to play for the evening service in the Baptist church. Maybe you like to go with us? We have Communion too tonight."

"Really?" she asked. "Do you think I would be welcome?"

"You sure would be," I said, trying to assure her.

Quickly she decided." If Claude drives my car, and I ride with you, then you two will take me home after dark! I'd love to go."

"I don't have a church here," she said sadly on the way to town. "I attend a the Presbyterian church in town now, because they need my help. Every year the church has a huge rummage sale and I had almost given your dishes to that church for charity."

I shuddered at the thought, wondering who would have been so lucky. "Mary, I am so glad you gave me that beautiful china. Thank you again," I looked at the small lady. Sensing her loneliness, I touched her hand.

"Who will take care of me when I get old?" she asked quietly.

Holding her tiny arm. we entered the church. Mary was soon greeting everyone, telling the head usher, " I feel right at home because every Sunday I listen to your service on the radio! This is my friend. Amy!" She introduced me as if I were the visitor.

Sitting in the pew, Mary was radiant, asking if we were members of the Baptist church.

"No," I told her. "We are guests too and attend the services. Our denomination does not have a church here either."

Comfortable with that answer, Mary enjoyed the fellowship. When communion was about to be served, she asked in a loud whisper. "Is it for me too?"

Her question could be heard by those sitting in the corners of the small building. "If you are ready to receive Christ's love, please join us," I answered in a soft reassuring voice.

"But I have never taken communion!" she said, listening intently to the words spoken by the minister. Nodding to herself, Mary made a decision when the bread was passed. She took it; and when the wine followed, she drank from the little glass cup. She kept holding it in her hand and smiled.

After the doxology she still held the little glass. "Do you think I may take this home for a souvenir? I love miniatures," she explained. Happy as a child, she carried the cup to the door, showing it to the friendly pastor. She thanked him for the lesson and added cautiously, "Amy told me to keep this cup for remembrance. It was good to be with you folks."

"You are welcome, and come again," the pastor said, shaking her hand. " God bless you Mary."

When I called the next day to ask Mary how she was feeling, I learned that she was gone. Mary had taken her last trip.

BEEE HAPPY!

When we made our plans to move far from town I hoped to be self sufficient and independent. It was one reason for growing our own vegetables and Claude being very fond of honey made me decide to start the bee culture of Apiary Science. Only one hive was my plan at first but that turned out different.

I had several hives when we arrived to live on Partridge Road. These are my hives. The bees do not interest Claude even though he loves honey. It is like with fishing it is my hobby. And he eats most of the fish, he cleans them too and I will fry the beautiful fillets for him.

Since our Social Security check was sent to Claude, and I had several years to wait before becoming eligible for that benefit, we planned to supplement our income by extending the number of bee hives to about fifty. And so I had become a commercial beekeeper.

Last year we produced over two tons of honey to refine and put into our jars.

Yes, with Claude carving beautiful signs and his organ playing we actually are living comfortably. My sales at the Farmers Market provides us with enough money to pay our property taxes.

Yes, its possible to earn your living in the U.P.

As a mother of many children I had not found time to learn a whole lot about bees. But I certainly had wide experience living in a beehive! Our white house down state had a queen mother and children running in and out in every direction. Children, like bees, eat a lot, sing a lot, and make a constant, happy noise.

For thirty years I was privileged to be the queen of such a hive. Our house even experienced swarming, the natural division that takes place when bees or children need more room to grow. Swarming also happens when the queen gets older. She may take part of her family and move to a place better suited to the needs of the hive.

Swarming is a planned procedure. Scouts are sent ahead to inspect a proper place for a new beginning, and when one is found, alas, some family members stay behind.

We followed the latter swarming pattern, and our scouts built us a beautiful home in the woods near Lake Superior where we find plenty of room to perform our joyous bee dance and make lots of honey. In short, the story of our family parallels the life of a bee colony.

Realizing how wonderful it would be to please my loving husband with golden drippings for his toast fresh from a honey comb, I first dreamed of owning just one hive with thousands of little workers bringing nectar and pollen from the wildflowers that abound in our woods. Yes, at fifty-four, I would become a bee keeper!

My dream began before we moved to the U.P., and because there are many bee science secrets to learn, I had to find a teacher. Fortunately, one mile behind our home, there lived a wise old beekeeper, Wilbur Vos. Inquiring about the size of a beehive and how to obtain its inhabitants, he responded with enthusiasm.

First, he told me I would need two hives so one colony could help the other. That seemed like good reasoning. We all need good neighbors. I learned there are several ways to populate a hive. One way is to buy a package of bees, queen and all, from a dealer. Wilbur explained that the package arrives by mail, and postal clerks don't wait long to tell you they're in!

Another way is to place an empty bee hive near several other colonies. A swarm may be tempted to move in. The attraction is free living, the pay comes later in the form of golden honey.

Third, you can divide a strong family by force, and the orphaned hive will grow a new queen by feeding a regular worker female eggs, royal jelly, and honey.

Fourth, the most exciting, you can capture a swarm. Being alerted by police, the Humane Society, or a worried mother who sees a cluster of bees bigger than a football hanging on a tree or bush near her children, you learn that a swarm has formed. This sounded so exciting I wanted to go out and catch a swarm right then.

However, thoughtful person that he was, Wilbur Vos wanted me to be sure I was serious about the bee business, so he invited me to his bee yards. Handing me some of his protective gear, he explained clearly that bees use one end for gathering nectar and the other for defense.

Wilbur, a quiet man, talks slowly but works fast. His "bee" was stretched to "beee!" He called one morning and said,, "Amy, beee ready for the beee work at nine-thirty. I'll beee at your home, and we'll beee at the beee yard by ten."

When Wilbur arrived I was ready! Dressed in double slacks, a shirt with a collar, plus two sweatshirts, those bees were not going to scare me. Wilbur noticed. He said in his calm way, "Amy, it'll be a nice day," meaning, you'll be too warm and appear scared. He gave me gloves and a hat with a veil. Although he had bare arms and hands, he too was wearing a veil. "Hate to get stung on the nose," he explained.

He lit the smoker, which had dried sumac fruits for fuel, and gave it to me. "And now you are my beee helper, Amy," he said, giving me also a hive tool which fit nicely in my hand.

Then he sat down on top of a beehive, letting the bees buzz all around his feet. He looked around calmly. "Beee keepers must be calm," he said, "You must look around and enjoy yourself."

"Let's see," he pondered. "That bee hive near the fence is a mean one; we'll save that one for last." Approaching the hive nearest him, he cracked the cover glued with propolis, then, lifting it slowly, told me, "Pump some smoke down in the hive!"

I saw the busy bee colony at work, lining the frames of the top super (tray) in orderly fashion. When the smoke calmed their activity, Wilbur care fully lifted one middle frame out of the hive, showing me the workers (females), the fat, happy drones (males), and finally the beautiful queen, "her Majesty!"

Almost reverently, he placed that frame again between the others. "We will have to give these a bigger home," he said. "It is a nice, hard-working family, but it's getting too big." He put a third story super on top of it. When a few bees crawled onto his arms and hands, he grinned, "These are my friends."

We "worked bees" that way until one-thirty when Wilbur told me it was lunch time. The noon rush hour over, we drove to a restaurant, parking our truck two blocks away. Walking down the road, Wilbur said, "I don't know why people are afraid of bees." Nor did I.

Already I was hooked on beekeeping. My kind and gentle teacher had made me forget that bees sting! Every week, sometimes twice, I was Wilbur's beee-helper and enjoyed a good lunch. He always found a new place to eat, parking the truck a distance from the restaurant, but it never failed, we always brought some bees with us. While we ate the salad, a bee would buzz to the light on the ceiling. Soon another and another would follow, and when two or three showed up, the ice cream sundae or coffee cup was emptied fast by the customers as they left. I was innocent. Anyone could have searched me. I was clean of bees, but Wilbur hummed. It was his pockets!

He wanted everyone to know that bees don't sting for fun, like mosquitoes or other insects. They're far too busy for that! They only sting to protect their colony. For that, they will give their lives.

My first family of bees arrived in the mail, and Wilbur helped me give them a new home in our back yard. He unceremoniously dumped the swarm into my hive, then took the queen in her cage, punctured a hole in the sweetened wax stopper, and placed it in between two frames.

Wilbur explained the process. "The workers will eat the sweet wax and release her." he said. "When they are used to her odor, they will accept her as one of the family. She will have her own ladies in waiting who'll comb her hair, keep her groomed, and feed her. All she needs to do is lay eggs, a thousand to fifteen hundred each day in the summer months."

Wilbur continued his lesson, "The queen will lay thousands of female eggs, which become the workers, and approximately five hundred male eggs, the drones that keep everyone happy or annoyed. Those boys eat a lot, they hum and buzz, but they don't work. In the fall, the workers have no patience with these lazy goof-offs, and one cold morning the girls stop them at the front door where they freeze to death."

Later that week, Wilbur phoned me. A small swarm had been located behind an old abandoned house. "I will teach you how to catch them," he added.

It looked simple. Unprotected, he held a wire basket under the branch where a cluster of bees waited for the scouts to report on a good location for a new hive. "Won't they sting?" I asked.

"No," Wilbur said. "Most people think swarming bees are dangerous, but each bee has her stomach full of honey that she takes from their old home to build a new honey comb. They're content and

83

full, and they have no place to defend yet!"

With a quick, strong shake, the bees fell into the basket, tumbling all over each other, closing in on the queen. Those which fell on the outside marched like soldiers to the entrance of a waiting hive. "By tomorrow, they will be organized ," Wilbur said. "Some will do housecleaning, others will protect the queen, and some go out in the field. Each bee has a special job to do."

It all looked so easy. I became excited when Wilbur told me one morning, "Amy, there's a big swarm hanging in a hawthorn tree behind a home. You're on your own. It's your chance to fill that second hive."

It was a beautiful day. Driving through town, the address was easy to find. I found the huge bee cluster hanging on the top branch. Wilbur had warned me to take a long ladder, but mine reached only halfway up. Two-inch thorns were everywhere. Investigating the tree, it seemed easy to climb, except for the thorns that would attack my veil. I was helpless. Disgustedly, I looked at the big swarm. The people who owned the house were either not home or pretending not to be. All at once, I spotted help nearby. It was noon, and a big yellow truck was parked next door while repairing the power line. The basket for lifting repair men up sat empty while the men ate lunch.

I approached the foreman and stated my dilemma. Would it be possible for one of your men to drive your truck under that Hawthorn and lift me up to that bee swarm?

"A swarm of bees? Thousands of bees?"

"Yes," I told him, "twenty thousand or more." A swarm weighs five pounds or more, and each pound has approximately four thousand bees."

Not on his life! replied the foreman. The bees might attack the truck or hang around in it for days.

One of the men asked, "You catch those lady?"

"Yes," I replied.

"For what?"

"For my hive, I am a beekeeper," was my proud answer.

A horrible thought came to the man's mind, "What if you don't catch them, lady?"

I was reading his mind, and adding to his worries, I said, "Any minute now they will take off, and I don't know where. When they go, they go! This is why I wear this veil!"

It was not long before the foreman said, "Let's help. I'll go inside the truck and move the basket. You guys all stay out of the way."

Never have I received more courtesy. Assisting me into that basket, he then drove under the swarm. I rode high, feeling like a queen myself, admired by the men. The swarm fell right into my wire cage, and I was lowered to the ground. Placing the cage in the trunk of my car, I closed the lid. When I thanked the men, they cheered. I had saved their lives. Later I gave each one of them a small jar of honey.

Through that summer and fall Wilbur patiently taught me the art of apiary culture, or beekeeping. He showed me how to handle everything from multiplying colonies and re-queening to harvesting the golden honey, which is, stealing the wealth of those hard working, ambitious colonies. Yes, Wilbur taught me to be a thief!

By August or early September we smoked the hives to drive the bees down then placed a trap in between the full super and took what we thought was our fair share. Sometimes we took as much as 150 pounds from one hive. Each frame with its honey, nine to ten frames in a box (or super) was neatly capped with wax. One by one the little nectar-filled hexagons were cured to perfection then sealed with wax.

In the ancient past this was the food of gods to be given in sacrifice or consumed by royalty. Honey was a delicacy thought to have special power to cure sickness of heart, soul, and mind.

A honeycomb is delicately built with approximately two-thousand little pockets on each side. It looks like these little containers are built to release their treasure when turned upside down, but not so. They are structured to hold the honey, curving inward and down, like little pockets.

One morning late in September Wilbur called. He spoke faster than usual. "Amy, will you help me to extract today?"

"Oh, yes," I replied, "Do I need protective clothing?"

"No, come right over," Wilbur said. "We will be busy today."

Wilbur's wife Letha greeted me with a smile. "Amy, I'm glad you're here! If Wilbur gives you time off, come in for coffee."

The long lane to the honey house was sheltered by big maples. I heard machinery clicking and motors humming. Wilbur was standing near a table skimming the wax from full frames of honey with a huge knife shaped like a two-edged sword. It looked easy. Wilbur explained that the knife was heated electronically. The wax fell on a heated grate and melted into beautiful yellow cakes.

Wilbur then placed the frames in what looked to me like a huge washing machine, a centrifuge to spin out the honey leaving the open wax cells to be used again next summer.

I am not technically inclined and I don't trust machinery, and I saw hundreds of bees everywhere buzzing madly or crawling helplessly on the floor. They did not appear to bother Wilbur.

"Don't they sting?" I asked.

"They are my friends, Amy," he replied.

I wasn't quite sure about the friend part, but I had not been stung all summer, having been careful to keep protected.

As Wilbur showed me how to uncap and slice the wax from a frame, the bees began to alert me to danger. I felt a crawling sensation inside the leg of my jeans and something fastening on my leg. A bee had found a cozy dark shelter, something like its home, and it kept crawling up my calf.

I stamped my foot: once, twice, three times. Wilbur was too busy to notice I thought. I tried a little dance, not very gracefully, then more of a foot stamping like a wooden shoe "Dutch klompen dance." Wilbur's little friend just seemed to enjoy it and hung on. Then it crawled up to my knee.

Wilbur asked me to empty a pail of honey, "Pure as gold," he said proudly. Bending to reach for the pail gave the bee more room and it crawled a couple inches above my knee. No dancing or stomping would help me now and knowing Wilbur's friend was trapped gave me the shivers.

Being a modest woman, it was impossible to catch the intruder, it was only a question of who would strike first, me to pinch or her to sting (only females sting). She won. I gave a soft squeal and a hard squeeze and it was all over for her, but not for me! Her stinger kept pumping the potent poison.

Pretending the sting was not there, I helped Wilbur where he needed me with bees still crawling all over the floor. I had to bend

86

once more to empty a pail, and it was then that I noticed that Wilbur had his socks pulled neatly over his pant legs. Why hadn't he told me?

After what seemed like hours, Wilbur said, "Amy, let's go see Letha. She may have coffee ready."

Too proud to limp, I followed Wilbur up the lane to his house. "Excuse me," I said, and I hurried to a secluded place where I could examine my swollen leg. The stinger was a very small black thorn, yet the damage lasted for weeks. But ever since, I have been immune to bee stings. Though it still hurts to be stung, I never swell.

Drinking our coffee Wilbur asked slowly, "Ever been stung by a beee, Amy?"

HAPPY BEES

A drowsy bee crawled from a crack in the black carton I had wrapped around the hive for extra protection against the below-zero temperatures of our Upper Peninsula winters. I watched the bee stretching her wings, happy that at least this colony had survived and was ready for spring cleaning. This one bee represented many which were ready to work.

Black dots peppering the snow showed evidence that worker bees were carrying the dead far from the hive for spring burial. The vigorous young bees were making room for a new generation of workers, or for happy, lazy drones. The queen now was laying thousands of eggs each day.

To keep the colonies happy, a beekeeper must check every hive for food supplies. Early spring becomes a treasure hunt, with the healthy golden bees cooperating, and it is a marvelous discovery. Through six months of snow, cold and blistering north winds the colonies have survived.

Some hives are found to have plenty of food, while others are not so lucky. In those, the bees cling to each other for help, hunger screaming at the door. Sprinkling a generous helping of sugar syrup on an empty comb restores the sad colony in a short time. Then every bee begins working again at a certain task, and the queen resumes her egg-laying job. Like families, every colony has its own characteristics. Some will work quietly, others are loud and noisy. There are colonies which have died en mass, as though a catastrophe had struck all at once. Often the cause of death cannot be explained. Plenty of food may be stored in a lower section, still all die of starvation. Bees move up, never down, for food in the winter, because the hive is warmer at the top section.

The reason for the death of one colony was easily explained. A field mouse had moved downstairs for the winter and raised her family cozy and comfortable in the warm hive. Because their noisy neighbors kept the bees awake during winter hibernation, the colony consumed its winter food too quickly and died. The intruders left behind a mess of broken frames, having eaten the sweet wax without paying their rent.

My colonies situated in a beautiful area at the Hendrickson farm enjoy bee heaven. Another dozen hives are located three miles east at the Luoma's place. Both farms have their own charm and benefits for beekeeping.

Carl and Ruth Hendrickson's farm is on sandy soil with fertile fields, hilly country where the Montreal creek wanders through the pastures. The beehives hidden behind a heavy evergreen hedge are sheltered from Lake Superior's cold wind. The morning sun quickly warms the chilly air.

Ruth and I are good friends. The best of friends. We share the same interest in nature and all that grows. But Ruth is very allergic to bee stings, so with millions of my bees at her doorstep, we must be friends!

Ruth is known county-wide for her flowers. Some neighbors call her "Ruth with the flowers." My bees have plenty of food, and Ruth feeds me too. She calls from the safe side of the hedge, "Amy, can you take a break? Lunch is ready!"

A bee yard can be a lonely place, because one receives few visitors with bees swarming in every direction. A beekeeper once told me, "I keep bees to get away from people; there's solitude for me in the field. There is peace. Nobody bothers me working with my bees!"

When Ruth calls, I am ready! And who else would tell me with a smile not to poke fun at her bee sting remedy? When I enter her kitchen to enjoy Ruth's lunch, I note that she has a thick slice of onion taped to her nose! She laughed at herself.

"I read about it in Prevention Magazine," she said. "A slice of onion on a bee sting will draw out the poison." She chuckled again and the onion slipped to one side of her nose, making me laugh uproariously!

"It seems to help " she said. "Last week Carl was stung on his neck and I tried it on him. He didn't swell up at all!"

Ruth looked too comical I couldn't keep a straight face. I asked, "How did it happen, Ruth?"

"This morning hanging out the wash, a bee pestered me." she

replied. "It was coming at me from the other side of the hedge. Finally, it had enough nerve to sting me. Carl took out the stinger, but it's a difficult place to keep that onion put." She laughed again, but rather sadly, for here eyes teared from the onion and the sting.

Carl joined us. "We're invited to a wedding tonight," he explained, giving his wife a concerned look.

"Oh," Ruth answered. "They'll recognize me. Don't worry, Amy," Ruth assured me that she would be fine at the wedding reception.

"Yeah, you musn't worry, Amy. I'll take her dancing tonight. Ruth looks fine to me, always does." Carl spoke as though to convince me but more so to encourage his wife.

At Joan Loumas' place I was not that lucky. One afternoon, David, the oldest son, met me. He was scowling. His hat was pulled low over his face and he did not answer my greeting. What he said sounded almost like swearing. Pretending not to understand, I walked into Joan's kitchen with a jar of honey, a gift for the use of their property for my apiary.

"Did you see David?" Joan asked. "Be careful! he's mad at you. Angry as a hornet!"

"That's what I thought." I said. " He seemed to swear at me. "Why?"

She snickered then burst out laughing, "David has a new girl friend, and she's very nice. Friday night he walked out behind the barn. We told him not to, but he did. A bee stung his lip and it swelled up terribly! That will teach him to stay away from those hives!"

"Do you want me to move the bees?" I asked anxiously. Their farm is on low ground with clay soil and bees do very well all summer, especially late in the fall when the clover and trefoil are in bloom.

Joan's husband Eugene arrived in the kitchen and heard my question. "What, move those bees? never!" Then he began laughing, too. "David had a hard time Saturday night, but they have planned another date this week. He really likes this girl, but kissing her last week was a problem. Well, he could, but there wasn't much taste to his kisses! It's a good test for the girl. Let them try again this week-end!"

Loving the little episode, Eugene warned me to stay out of David's path. "He'll not forget this for a long time, a very long time!" he said.

"Don't you dare move those hives!" Joan said. "I haven't ever grown more tomatoes or pickles."

Joan is a real pickler. She slices, cubes, and pickles them whole, hundreds of jars every year. "Amy, those pickle vines don't quit. They produce bushels and bushels. It must be your bees, eh? We used to re-seed clover in one field every three years, but since you brought your bees here, we've not been doing it. Those fields are beautiful!"

"Do bees pollinate clover, too?" she asked. "David will just have to stay away from your hives, that is all!"

Smiling, I left for the barn. Yes, the Luomases are good friends too.

In springtime a beekeeper must encourage the colonies to be strong so that thousands of female workers will develop in time for summer production. Summer days are busy for both the bees and the apiarist. Section after section of supers must be added weekly in honey flow season, July through September. In the fall comes harvesting; we call it robbing. Yes, it is stealing, but we're not alone. Others come to rob our bees, too.

Skunks will eat bees by the thousands in one night. Tapping lightly on the entrance board, the bees crawl sleepily to see who's knocking, and the skunks grab handfulls of hapless bees and eat them as if they were candy!

A queen may lay two thousand eggs a day; a skunk may eat four thousand bees in a night, and soon the colony is dying, the work force unable to keep up the demand for new supplies.

Trying to catch the skunk with a Havahart trap is at times frustrating. The angry bees may kill the enemy in the trap but many will lose their lives in the process because the stinger part of the bee's reproductive system is left in the skunk's hide.

One time, while retrieving a trap, the angry bees took me for the enemy, attacking furiously. Covered with bees, I ran to the evergreens to lose my scent by rubbing myself with pine branches. This may have saved me from the fate the skunk suffered during the night.

91

Warm August evenings will carry the fragrance of curing honey to the woods and swamps for miles around. When the evening air is moist, the sweet smell tempts black bears that must eat ravenously to store fat for their long winter sleep. Usually shy and avoiding people, bears will take risks for honey and fat bee larvae.

We have hidden for hours under the stars near a corn field waiting for a night visitor that did not show up. A bear that has tasted honey will return again and again, but once having been caught in a trap, the smart animal will remember not to be trapped again. Usually lights and noise will make a bear run, and hopefully not return.

But bears remain a threat to the hives. One night we stood watch as the ground fog rose from the creek and stars appeared one by one. Then the sky changed almost to pitch black and we saw a black shadow moving slowly, step by step through the mist. The bear seemed to be enormous. He lifted his head, listening, looking, sniffing the air. We watched the huge animal approaching the row of beehives.

Like lightning he struck a hive, grabbing one section and walking upright, the bear disappeared down the hill to the swamp. We had failed! The bear was smarter than we were. There was nothing to do but light the smoker and try to calm the remaining angry bees. Picking up a broken brood box and replacing the frames in the wee hours of a new day, we promised ourselves to outsmart the night visitor the next time, but by then the old bear's taste may have changed to sweet corn or oats.

Sometimes we win, however. Ruth Hendrickson's call one morning brought relief. "We had our visitor again last night, Amy. We heard lots of noise. There's a bear in the live trap!"

We had baited the trap with bacon grease, candy bars, and, a broken frame with honey and fat bee larvae for a tempting dessert, and we won. The DNR hauled our pesky friend away to be released in the far woods.

Almost every year, however reluctantly, we must share our golden bounty with our wild neighbors. Often they are smarter than we. It's all part of country living in Michigan's Upper Peninsula.

FARMERS' MARKET

I love to grow things! I love to plant and cultivate, then watch my garden mature. I will caress a cabbage, especially a fine Savoy head, with leaf veins like those on an old lady's hand. Sometimes while greedily gathering my bounty, I pause to hug a fat squash, or kiss a prime Jack Be Little pumpkin.

My colorful gourds make old ladies and little children happy. I sell them for a nickel each, and men smile and dig an extra coin from their pockets to please their wife or child.

That bulldozer operator who predicted my soil would never grow a garden was proven wrong. Soon I grew more than Claude and I could use, and since city folks like fresh vegetables, we joined our neighbor growers at the county farmer's market. Each Saturday from late July to frost, I proudly display nature's gifts from my garden, love gifts from good Mother Earth.

The people of St. John's Church walked slowly down the aisle to the door. The church was almost filled to capacity.

Claude, my husband, forcefully played the postlude, a variation of "A Mighty Fortress." There is a lot of volume in that old pump organ, which he works with his feet as much as with his fingers.

The hymn came rolling out to the pastor, a stocky man, as he shook hands with his people to the rhythm of Claude's joyful playing. Sitting there on the end of a pew, the words to his music flowed through my mind, when Irma Mattson pointed her nose in my direction. Coming close, she asked in a loud whisper, "Amy would you sell me some small pickles?" "Pickles?" I asked. The Mighty Fortress faded away. Pickles! Here in God's house I was reminded of my earthy vocation.

"Yes," she nodded. "Do you have some?"

"I will look and call you tomorrow. Irma."

That morning as I came to church, Laura Makela had been waiting for beets. On Saturday she had cornered these in Penney's store and said she needed some pickling beets. Her seeds had not germinated this spring, she said.

It seems when people see me, they envision good things to eat!

It all began the day John Sola called me. "Amy," he said, "Have you heard of the Farmer's Market? We sell almost anything good to eat, but we have no honey. We would like you to bring your honey and any extra vegetables you may have to sell. The market is held on Saturday mornings."

"Sounds good," I told him. "We have honey, carrots, beets, swiss chard, pumpkins, squash, parsley and all that."

"Bring them!" John said. "You will have some fun."

The marketing experience was new for me. I had been giving away my extra produce to my friends or to Barbara, our goat. I was not at all acquainted with pricing or how to display my wares.

On Saturday at about 9:30 I arrived at the market place and set up a table with a neat golden-yellow tablecloth to match the beautiful honey and I laid out a display of my produce.

When I finished and looked over to my neighbor's stand, I became horrified. Her table was a beautiful arrangement of bright red beets, washed with the "tails" clipped; orange carrots clean and shiny in neat bunches, beans in plastic bags, and swiss chard so big and fresh you would love to eat it raw. She had a price list taped to her truck and gave me a friendly smile.

When I looked at my hairy carrots it was as if I had forgotten to shave my legs! And the tails of my beets drooped over the edge of the sloppy table. That first day was a disaster, but it took only one week to learn!

The next Saturday I stood with pride behind my stand. The golden yellow tablecloth looked neat enough. Indeed, the display of fresh produce and honey plus home-made jelly made my table into a "horn of plenty" but people passed me by.

The price was right. What now? Did nobody trust me?
John Sola encouraged me. "You have a very nice table, Amy."

Claude, somewhat skeptical of this new adventure, stopped by to see how I was doing. "I'm not selling much," I confessed, "everyone is nice, but they don't buy."

He gave it to me straight, "Amy, your table looks nice but too expensive with that table cloth and all. And you are dressed in a white blouse. Wear some regular clothes." He was right.

This has been my seventh summer at the Farmer's Market and folks now recognize me. To some I am "the honey lady;" to others, "the pickle woman," but all of them are friends.

We PRO-ducers, as John Sola calls us, have our own specialty. Mine is honey and a variety of herbs and greens. We who sell at the market are friends, perhaps because our prices are uniform. There is no competition except in quality.

One Saturday, a young mother approached me. She complimented me saying, "It seems you are very healthy." Then glancing at my table, she said, "I would like to eat what you grow; you're an advertisement for your produce." Some of the greens were unfamiliar to her and by telling her how to prepare the simple dishes, we became friends. There is no doubt she is healthy now.

It has become my habit to give out recipes. A friendly, elderly man told me his wife was not well and he was cooking for himself. Waiting until most of the customers had left, and taking notes, he wrote down my instructions for preparing the summer squash he had purchased. His friendly smile meant more than the change in my hand.

Oh, there are some who have complaints. Viola Bracket is a pickler. For weeks I supplied her with ice cream buckets full of pickles not over three inches long, as she requested. I measured the first two every summer; later I know. She cubes, slices, grinds and preserves cucumbers whole. She makes 13th day sweet pickles, a long process. They must become crisp or they're no good.

One morning she phoned me, and her voice was crisp! "What kind of pickles did you sell me?" she barked. "My pickles went limp." Her complaint continued, "It is a lot of work, and I added the hot syrup on the 13th day as I was supposed to, but all my pickles are limp! Did you sell me some small Straight-eight Slicers?"

"No, I don't grow that kind," I replied. "I only grow County Fair pickling cukes, Viola "

"Well, but these went limp. I will have to throw them out. I called the County Agriculture Agent, too, and do you know what he asked me? 'Have you ever pickled before?' Amy, I've made pickles for forty years, bushels and bushels of pickles, and he dared to ask me that?"

Viola's tirade continued, "His advice did not help much, either.

He gave me a lot of literature. Are you sure these were the right cukes, Amy?"

"Yes, Viola, I'm sure." I tried to be friendly, but her growl was awful.

The following Saturday I saw her coming, a basket on her arm and a sun-bonnet to protect her skin. She asked for sweet corn and picked out the best; she squeezed my pickles and bought more. "How much?" she asked.

Now it was my turn I thought, then charged her fifty cents extra for the corn and a dollar more for the pickles. We have been friends ever since, the price is normal again, and her pickles are crisp.

Our weather here in the U.P. is a great factor for our success on Saturday morning. Gerhard Olson has told me he prays for sunshine from 9:30 to 11:30 a.m. on Saturdays because those are the best market hours. Gerhard is a devout man and usually we could not complain, but lately we have lost faith in him, for it seems that he has taken matters into his own hands.

Gerhard fabricated a fancy yellow tarp that hooks onto his truck and extends over his table far enough to shelter those who stop there. He did it so his vegetables stay fresh, he tells us, but we have noticed that it rains more often now on Saturday mornings. We suspect he has been praying for rain. His customers chat with him under that tarp and buy his beautiful carrots and beans at the same time. It's a cozy set-up, but it isn't fair!

Half the fun of the Farmer's Market is in the people you come to know. For example, Uno Mattson comes to the market to shop for his wife, Irma. He has been down state to Lansing, and that is why she approached me in church. "See, Amy," she said, "Uno is the best sauna stove maker in our area, and they're reasonable, too."

When I brought her the small pickles she requested, Uno had just returned from the University in East Lansing. It had been a big trip for him; he was gone for ten days, showing the folks at the Lansing Art Festival how to build a good sauna stove.

He took rocks with him from Lake Superior near Little Girls Point, good rocks, not rocks that pop and crack when you splash water on for steam. They showed me pictures of Uno at the festival working on his stove.

Uno always wears a railroad cap with the visor turned up and always has a big smile for everyone. He is a happy man, and important to us. How could we ever be clean way down to the pores of our skin if we did not have Uno to make our sauna stoves? When he comes to market next Saturday, I'm certain he will bring the pictures with him so we all will be sure he was there in Lansing representing our U.P. And it was all paid for by the festival! Irma told me so.

We have our rules for the market set by the manager John Sola. One of the hardest rules allows no selling before 10 a.m. At 9:45, a crowd will gather, each person coming for a certain item. The day's hot item is a fruit or vegetable which ordinarily is not quite ripe. July tomatoes? Sweet corn the first of August? Not in our beautiful, cool U.P! September tomatoes, maybe, if there is no frost.

Small pickles are another problem. Cukes will grow ten inches in a day, if only to confuse the pickle picker. So folks come early and beg, "Could you sell now, only for me? I can't wait, have lots to do."

The last ten minutes is torture for consumers and sellers. We used to let people choose what produce they wanted and stuff it in a shopping bag, then when John Sola rang his cowbell and shouted, "OK, go ahead. Sell!" customers would reach out one hand with the money and grab their bag of produce with the other. This year we have a new rule: No bagging!

But begging goes on, with eyes fixed on that nice cabbage or cauliflower or the best bunch of beets. The question lurks in every mind, "Who will get first choice?"

To ease the tension, some have found a way which is not against the rule. They lay a fat squash, a nice bunch of parsley, or a couple cukes on the ground. They stand behind them at attention, toes pointed, guarding their treasures until John gives the signal. There is a mad rush as a cuke is added at the last minute and we lose count of dimes and cukes, but who cares? It is fun.

In approximately 30 minutes our selection is gone. A few stragglers pass by. No beans left? How come? No sweet corn! Why? All that's left are a few squash and big cucumbers. Then when we visit and exchange hopes and dreams. We proudly introduce relatives and children visiting from down state and share information. "This is my son. He lives in Grand Rapids and is an engineer. My daughter, she's a teacher and has four children."

Our Farmer's Market is what markets have been for centuries all over the world: Europe, China, Africa, and here in our beautiful U.P. The market provides for our basic needs, including friendship.

John Sola is right. We are all "PRO-ducers."

QUEEN BARBARA

I might as well do some shopping and make a deposit at the bank." I told Claude. "Will you help me get Barbara in the truck? It's time for her annual breeding vacation.

Claude mumbled something about that stubborn goat.

I made a list, signed some checks, and prepared a few birthday cards for the mail. When I was ready, Claude had gone to the woods.

With some grain and a few maple branches, Barbara's favorite food, I tricked her and she hopped on the gate of the truck, I gave her a push and locked her in.

Off we drove. The twelve miles to town was no pleasure trip for Barbara. I heard her move about nervously, stamping her feet on the metal floor as I got to the bank drive-in window.

"I see you have a special passenger," the teller said. He looked curiously at my goat from his small cubicle. "She's cute" he said.

"Oh, yes," I told him. Then I heard her marbles pattering on the floor of our new truck. "She is making a deposit too." I told him cheerfully.

His eyes popped but he didn't give me a receipt.

Claude will kill me for forgetting to put that old tarp on the floor and he'll make me clean up that mess too.

Barbara our goat is well aware of her importance to our little kingdom in the woods. She is of royal lineage, being the daughter of Narna. Because of Barbara, some people call our place, "The house of goat's milk and honey." now.

I learned about Narna one morning while browsing the want ads in the Ironwood Globe. An ad said, "Milking goat for sale, $35 cash." The price was so reasonable, Claude and I began talking seriously about buying her.

The next day I drove to the address given in the ad and met Narna's owners. I found they were a family that had moved from the Chicago area to the U.P., thinking to live off the land with the help of a goat, some chickens, and a pig. Narna was to be their lawn mower and supplier of milk. But when the first November snowstorm made it necessary to buy hay for Narna, the family was ready to return to the big city.

Narna was a pure bred Saurman goat. Though she had no horns, she was really beautiful, with long, silky, white hair. The children playing on a dirt floor of the cabin cried when they realized they were losing their friend. Feeling sorry for the family, I gave them fifty dollars and left feeling extremely rich; not because I was now the owner of a fine goat, but because I had never known the poverty I saw in that family.

When I brought Narna home and Claude discovered I didn't know how to milk a goat, he had second thoughts. "How do you plan to learn?" He asked.

"She was purchased at a farm in Saxon where they breed Saurman stock," I replied. "I'll just call and ask if they will give me lessons."

"It's your goat," he said and retired to his shop. Claude doesn't worry about problems. He just turns them over to me. At six the next morning I was at the goat farm near Saxon.

"Yes," the farmer's wife told me, "we sold Narna to the folks from whom you bought her. She is a nice goat, but not show stock."

In one session I learned to milk a goat. It was slow going until the lady told me her teats would fill again after a short release. "Don't pull, squeeze the milk out as if it were a balloon."

"This thing is not made of rubber," I protested, "it's alive!" But it helped to think of it that way, and I was glad goats have only two teats. What if I'd bought a cow?

I was back home by eight and practiced milking Narna again. "Give her grain and she'll stand still for you," the goat lady had said. It was true. Narna ate lots of grain that first week.

The goat lady also advised me to have Narna bred in November. Because inclement weather might prevent getting her to the buck when it was her breeding time.

"How do I know when she's ready, and where do I have her bred?" I asked.

"Just like humans," the lady laughed. "She'll wave her tail a lot. Then it's time to bring her. We charge twenty- five dollars for servicing, and if it doesn't work the first time, then ten dollars, and so on."

Claude and I always discuss major expenses, and this time he was apprehensive. "Seems to me it would be more economical just to buy milk," he grumbled. What is goat's milk like?" He came to like goat's milk far more than cow's milk!

Through the U.P. grapevine I learned of another goat person. She had come with her husband from the Chicago area to retire. They had brought a little goat kid to compensate for the grandchildren they'd left behind. Their goat was an Alpine, slender with a dark brown coat.

They were excited to meet me and congratulated me for having bought Narna. The man told me he'd made a luxurious home for their two goats. It was not just a barn, but a divided building with a living room where a radio played western music and polkas. They even had a play area in the bedroom and a bunk for each animal, so they could sleep separately.

"We are thinking of installing cable TV," the woman laughed. "In the morning we prepare peanut butter sandwiches and the goats come to the kitchen to get them. Your Narna will be welcome here."

"But do you know when it is the right time?" she asked.

"Let me show you a trick." She went to her bedroom and brought out a red handkerchief which she rubbed on the underside of the bucks belly. Then she put it in a plastic bag, and I was glad. Phew!

She told me each morning to show the cloth to your Narna.

"If she is indifferent, there is no use bringing her here to Noah. But when she begins to smell the cloth and gets excited, come immediately.

"Noah"? I asked.

"Yes. All our animals have biblical names. This goat is Esther, that one Rebecca."

"We gave our sheep New testament names," her husband added. "There is Peter and Paul, and there is Lydia. Remember her?" "Yes," I replied, "Lydia, the seller of fine linen and purple silk. But how much do you charge for Noah's services?" Given the goat's fancy quarters, I feared a luxurious price. But they assured me that Noah's services were free.

A few weeks later Narna waved her tail at the red handkerchief and I had no doubt she was asking for a visit with Noah. Having no further need for the hanky, I returned it with a thank you.

Five months later Claude phoned while I was at our goat friends' house for a Bible study. (Did I hear Noah snicker?) "Amy, come quickly," Claude said. "Narna has delivered two kids, and there may be a third one." He sounded helpless, as men are in such situations.

Rushing home, I found Claude was right. Narna was a busy mother, licking two brown kids, both bucks. Then I saw a I third kid lying in a corner, wet and helpless, her white hair matted. Evidently Narna had forgotten she had delivered three kids.

The little tyke, a doe, was cold and miserable; too weak to lift her head. I carried he gently inside and rubbed her down with a fluffy bath towel, then gave her warm milk from a bottle. The little goat tried to stand, but her hind legs seemed too long. They buckled. Finally, she gave up and dragged herself along with her front legs. Trying to help, I made splints to support her weight, which made her look as though she was walking on stilts.

Meanwhile, the two bucks were dancing crazy eights and jumping all over the barn.

"The little doe needs more help," I told Claude. I phoned the veterinarian, Dr. Barbara Bolich, for advice.

"So Narna had triplets!" she said. "Bring her in to the office with her kid. She may be ruptured after a difficult birth. I'll look at her, too."

Narna turned out to be well, and the doctor examined the weakling. "You had the right idea, Amy. I'll put a professional splint on the legs. Come again in three days. These problems often correct themselves, but we must make sure."

"What's this going to cost?" Claude asked, thinking again that it would be more economical to buy milk.

"You penny pincher!" I scolded! Is this your thanks for Narna's good milk? You're pouring it on your oatmeal every morning and drinking a quart every day. And you worry about a doctor's bill!"

The last office call was encouraging. The little doe was walking on her own. "What did you name her?" The vet asked.

"She has no name yet," I said. "I was not sure I would be able to keep her. Goats should jump and dance and turn somersaults. I wasn't sure she ever could."

"Well you better give her a name. She will do all that and

102

more," the doctor assured me.

Now I must ask her for the bill, I thought. I figured three office calls and Narna's checkup could cost at least fifty dollars. Then I had a thought: What if I named the kid after Doctor Bolich? Would she give a discount?

"Why don't I name her Barbara, after you?" I asked, then added, "No, it wouldn't be right to name a crippled goat for a veterinarian."

"She will not be crippled, and I would be honored," Dr. Bolich said.

"Then I'll name her Barbara Joy; Joy being my middle name. What do I owe you?"

"I don't charge for my name sake!" she told me.

Dr. Bolich gladly accepted the half gallon of honey I had brought for her and I drove happily home with Barbara Joy. "She will be the queen of our place," I told Claude. It was wrong to say that in front of Barbara, because if ever there was a proud stubborn goat, is must be her.

Barbara is now nine years old, past middle goat age, and she has given us and our grandchildren hours of fun, producing many kids, and faithfully providing Claude with milk.

Since it was not advisable to have her bred with father Noah, we had to find a new buck. So each November Barbara vacations at a farm near Saxon for approximately two weeks with a goat named Adam in exchange for a gallon of honey. Adam is a Nubian, a goat with sad drooping ears, sad eyes, but a fine lusty buck. Barbara has never failed to become a mother five months after each vacation.

The mixed parentage always gives us brown buck kids, but the does are like Barbara, pure white. Last year she delivered a white does kid with one ear standing out like hers, but the other drooped like her father Adam. The little kid would shake her head, but the one ear would not go down, and the other would not stand up. We named her Flop, and I gave her to my friend Carol Harmon who lives near Little Girl's Point on Harmony Acres. Flop still shakes her head as if asking, "Why me?"

Barbara's popularity with town folks and visitors is boundless. She is the most pictured goat in the country. Recently, she was video taped and seen in living rooms from coast to coast, always ready to pose with dignity and with dignitaries. People ask about Barbara on

Christmas cards. One wrote, "Barbara was our famous star at our Thanksgiving celebration. She made our trip an unforgettable experience!" Only once did Barbara create a real problem. Visiting my father in Holland on his ninetieth birthday, I told him what a good fortune is was to have a goat like Barbara. Concerned he asked, "Amy do you need financial help? I've saved some money over the years."

"Dad we have plenty. Keep it for yourself," I replied.

"You always wanted to be independent," Father continued, "that's why you left for America. You're too proud, Amy. I did not know you were poor. I always thought every one in that country is rich. Do you really have to drink goat's milk?" He sadly shook his head.

I then remembered the Holstein cows grazing in the lush meadows in Friesland Province where I was born. To my father, a goat is a poor man's cow.

It took years before I came to understand why Barbara's mother Narna was not of show stock. She had what goat farmers call a poorly attached udder. It hangs very low. That's why our visitors often ask if Barbara gives lots of milk. Others say, "Amy, will you please milk her? Barbara seems to be uncomfortable!"

"No," I reply, "Barbara has just inherited a low slung udder. One of our grandchildren put it bluntly. "Grandma, I don't like that wibble wobble hanging on your goat."

Barbara still has a slight limp. When she was young, that twist made her walk a little sexy, but now it is a distinct wobble. Yet, for an old nanny goat, she can be extremely fast, especially when she spies a fine head of broccoli in my garden, her favored vegetable. I've lost that race with her several times, and I think she has begun to understand some mildly profane Dutch!

Once more this past spring Barbara became a mother. It was on a below zero day in late March. Several times I checked her, and late on a Saturday night her kid was born, head first. A goat kid should come feet first with its leather shoes showing and the head nestled neatly between its knees. But this time a little dark head dangled from the birth canal. Barbara talked soothingly to her baby and all went well. She delivered a little buck and began to lick it dry with her tongue. I had wanted a doe so I could retire Queen Barbara to green pastures near our pond.

"To be an expensive real life ornament?" Claude had sneered.

"But I congratulated Barbara, postponed her retirement, and told her, "Next year you must give me a nice white doe." One Sunday morning Claude called me early. "Amy your baby goat is dying,"

I had fixed a bed for the kid in the house. He was not dead yet, but very cold and miserable. Sitting near the stove in the living room, I rubbed the little guy until it was warm. I gave him some of Barbara's warm milk from a bottle and watched him recover. A mischievous look in his big black eyes seemed to say, "I'm by no means dead!"

In an hour he tried to walk. He was unstable at first, but soon he began to jump and finally got the rhythm and performed the Dance of the Wild Cucumber.

Goats are fun!

Sometimes we take Barbara to the cabin at Eel Lake. One summer we had set up an old tent for her stall. It is more for our convenience than Barbara's, for each morning we have fresh milk for Claude's oatmeal, and we don't have to hurry home to milk her, but can stay over night.

People fishing near the cabin often think they see a deer, but then we hear someone ask, surprised, "Is that a goat?

Barbara did surprise a young game warden who came walking out of the woods. We think he had been spying on us.

"How's fishing?" "Fine" we answered.

Then he told us about an occasional sighting of albino deer in the Ottawa Forest. "Our senator in Lansing has introduced a bill in congress to protect these animals" he said, rather officiously.

At that moment Barbara walked from her tent, looking with disdain at the officer. She kicked up her legs and ran to the lake for a drink.

The officer stared at our albino deer for a long time before he left.

IT'S SPRING!

We have heard it said, "there is no spring in the U.P., only two seasons: winter and the Fourth of July."

Not so! Spring may come early or late; it may last one day and leave for weeks, but then it comes again. This may happen two or three times. And then sometimes winter returns in May.

"Drip...drip...drip. Kaplunk, kaplunk, plunk!"

This morning splattering, dripping drops are everywhere. From the roof of our house rain drops plunk and sprinkle the back porch deck. From the hemlocks in front of the house quiet drops trickling down the feathery branches make a dull rustling as they hit the wet snow still covering the ground.

In this late March concert of dripping spring music, the constant clinkity clink of maple trees dripping the life- giving liquid into buckets is the sweetest sound of all, assuring us we have persevered through another cold winter here in Michigan's Upper Peninsula.

Hundreds of thousands of drops are making gallons and gallons of fresh sap. Soon our people will be boiling this down to golden maple syrup. It is spring time, sap running time!

"Halftail" our squirrel, rejected by his relatives and friends, knows it is sap time, too. Leaping up and down the trunk of the small maple in front of our home, he greedily licks the bark, going up and coming down he licks, enjoying his spring tonic so much we can almost hear him smacking his lips.

The maple has begun her spring ritual of lifting the life- giving sap to the highest branches after the long winter rest. Dulled by months of below zero temperatures and severe winter storms, we need to be restored too. The rhythm of the dripping makes us eager with Halftail for a taste of that sweet sap. Yes, we are greedy, like our squirrel.

Early this morning, my husband Claude, found the tools for drilling holes in our large maples for two dozen spiles, the hollow tubes with a hook attached to be driven into the sunny side of the tree.

We can't get enough of this delicacy, and it is free!

Like Halftail, we are excited, we know it is spring, but we want it sweeter, so we boil thirty gallons of sap down to one gallon of golden syrup on our wood stove in the kitchen. As it boils the maple fragrance fills our home. We can't wait to taste the nectar and make tea, or cool it for a sweet drink.

In the morning we add oatmeal to the hot liquid. a natural-flavored, wholesome, breakfast feast. Yes, Halftail,it's a spring meal, and spring makes animals, birds, and people a bit crazy. We become exuberant, happy, and daring; we do silly things. We're all a bit--sappy!

A scratching noise inside our wood stove tells us something is wrong. Opening the door, an odd-looking bird flies out toward the early light in the window. The red spot on its head tells me it's our hairy woodpecker wearing his tuxedo. He is dressed for his wedding with black tie and white shirt, now a rumpled mess. Clinging to the curtains, he did not look like the neat groom he wanted to be, trying to impress his future bride..

Nervously rocking a rolling beat on our metal chimney, he had apparently fallen into that black hole to the bottom of our stove. Catching him, we sent the hapless groom to a quick bath in a mud puddle, knowing he will soon return to his lofty instrument and the wedding will not be postponed. Spring is love; reckless, unashamed madness.

We hardly had finished breakfast when we heard more screeching and scratching in the kitchen. Something kept knocking on the fireplace damper, desperately scratching at the double flue of the chimney. Dismantling the stove pipe from the old cook stove, Claude faced a startled masked head. Green eyes peering angrily at him from that dark flue.

"A raccoon!" my husband said. "But it is not coming out." Apparently confusing the blackened chimney for a hollow tree, the coon did not want to come down and did not know how to climb up to the roof.

"Give it something to eat," I suggested, my motherly instinct wanting to feed the lonely and lost.

"Feed it? We'll have to catch it first!" Claude said. Foreseeing a

107

raccoon-chase around our dining room table, he added, "It is best to set a Havahart trap in front of the chimney opening. Do we have smelt left?"

Taking a good generous portion of the little fish for bait, he placed the trap on top of the old-fashioned warming ovens of the cookstove, a relic left behind in a hunting camp on our property and restored to its former glory in our home. "I am hoping that the coon will soon be tempted." Claude said.

We forgot the trap while working outside. The dripping of maple sap continued all day. Several times I collected the precious liquid, refilling the kettles on our stove, the evaporating process leaving a lingering, sweet smell in our home.

We were expecting a missionary who was speaking at a conference in the Baptist church to be our guest for the weekend. Claude is the organist for several churches in our area, making us a target for hospitality. A variety of clergy have visited our home in the woods.

Late in the afternoon, I hurried once more to our sugar maples to empty the pails before sunset. In early morning it was easy to navigate around the trees. Then the frozen crust on the snow, still two or three feet deep, will support a person carrying two heavy pails of sap. But when the sun has attacked the snow through the day, one must be careful not to sink in a messy wet snowdrift.

Dressed in a warm jacket for the evening chill and wearing heavy boots, I carefully dragged the containers filled with foaming sap to the driveway cleared of snow. I noticed two men approaching me from behind the evergreens in front of our house. One was the pastor of the Baptist church, and the other, no doubt, our missionary guest.

At the very instant I looked up, one of my legs sank in the wet snow while the other stayed up. "Sorry, sorry!" the missionary said. "May I help?"

"No! No!" I shouted. I could see him pulling that trapped leg.

Realizing it would be much safer for him to stay on solid ground, the man said, "Oh, excuse me!"

Not quite sure of himself. the Baptist pastor explained,. "As I was telling you, brother, this is a very interesting place to visit."

"Please go inside," I begged. "My husband Claude will make you welcome."

Trying not to spill a drop of precious sap, I managed to keep my balance. I watched the men disappear in the direction of our home, leaving me to wrestle from the precarious grip of winter's residue. Both arms were useless, for attempting to push up only results in sinking deeper, nosediving in the soft snow. Sitting down and trying to free the trapped leg, then rolling to more solid footing is the only way out. When I finally made it to the house. wet and miserable, with my ten gallons of sap. the pastor introduced our guest who undoubtedly was embarrassed for not lending a helping hand to a fallen woman.

Graciously, our guest, Mr. Peterson, reached out for a forgiving handshake and remarked on the beautiful setting of our home in the woods. His comments about the pond with ducks and the beautiful spring day were soon interrupted by a loud Krrr, Krrr.

Jumping from his chair with a startled cry, the civilized preacher exclaimed,. "What can this be? An animal?"

"Sorry! I forgot, Sir," Claude said. "We must finally have caught our raccoon. It tumbled into the chimney last night and I set a trap this morning. The sap is running today and we were so busy, I forgot to check it."

Wildly thrashing and cussing in coon language and making lots of noise, the animal told us of his feelings. Black with soot and angry the raccoon resembled a furious little devil. Our guest speaker retreated to his bedroom to dress for the evening service and to find his composure.

Claude decided to take the animal in its cage with us as we drove to the meeting at the church, releasing it somewhere in the woods to continue its spring escapades miles from our place.

The next morning, Mr. Peterson, having rested well and being a dedicated and interested person, went with Claude to a men's breakfast. Returning later, he was telling us of the fine day he had with the pastor and his wife in town. "But I noticed something with a large bushy tail slipping under your front deck" he said. "Could it be another raccoon?"

"It may be. That first raccoon would have a long way to travel home," Claude said. "I promise to set another trap, this time near the front door."

On Sunday morning we again found a raccoon cussing at our doorstep and crying for help. On our way to church we released it in the woods between Lake Superior and town, hoping it would find its friend.

By now Mr. Peterson was not sure about being a guest at a home so deep in the U.P. forest. "Do you have bears here too? Do they come to your house?" he asked.

"Yes, we do," Claude said, "and at this time in the spring bears wake from hibernation and are hungry."

But I assured our guest, "Bears are harmless, unless you meet a mother bear who is protecting her cubs. Bears may look clumsy and slow when they tramp the woods, but don't be fooled! They can run fast." I told him of the hollow elm near our road that had been a home to a young bear the previous summer.

Enjoying his Sunday meal after completing his speaking engagements, Mr. Peterson was not as worried. Resting in Claude's easy chair, he slept for at least an hour. While he slept, Claude and I went out to our sugar maples to collect more of the free spring tonic.

Then we were startled by the sound of crying, and we discovered that our Barbara our goat, queen of our place in the woods, had just provided us with one more weekend surprise. She had given birth to triplets, two girls and a boy!

With her long warm tongue Barbara was busily drying the soft white hair of the two boy babies, while the girl, small and wet, lay in a corner trying to hold up her wobbly head.

Since the poor thing had been born last and needed help, I carried her into the living room to the warm stove, wrapping her in a bath towel and rubbing her as dry as Barbara would have done. Warmed, the infant goat quickly began to feel frisky. When one ear perked up and the other flopped sideways, we named her Flop.

Soon she was looking for food and licking my fingers. Letting me know I was fooling her, she cried, "Maaa, Maaa."

His nap disturbed, Mr. Peterson rose from his chair. "A baby?" he asked, rubbing his eyes as if he'd had a bad dream.

"Yes, we have become grandparents while you were taking a nap," I told him. "Two girls and a boy. Mother Barbara and kids are all doing well!"

He seemed unimpressed. There were no congratulations, no sign of interest or compliments. He'd had more surprises in one spring weekend than he could handle, poor man. Tired of cussing wild creatures, crying goat kids, and bears that might awake from their long U.P. winter sleep at any time, he was eager to return to the city.

We drove the missionary to the airport that evening, and the following week he flew to South America to search for lost sheep. Perhaps we deserve a little credit for his success due to the last-minute spring training we provided at our home in the woods.

THE SEASONS AT OUR EEL LAKE CABIN

Fall

 Dean Young built Eel Lake cabin to be a hunting camp, a deer hunting camp for him and his friends. In the U.P. it was accepted that women (like Dean's wife Mary and her sister Gladys) were not welcome in camp during deer season. Then Eel Lake cabin was man's domain. When Mary sold the cabin to us, we came upon two reminders of those deer hunts which we preserved in honor of Dean and his friends.

One was a deer head, a buck with a beautiful, symmetric, eight-point rack, Dean's prize trophy. The animal must have kept a sense of humor to his dying day, for it wore a silly grin. We named him Smiley.

The other reminder was a bottle of whiskey with about two fingers left. That reminder, however, disappeared. I hid the bottle one time when a Baptist minister friend asked to rent the cabin for a few days, and I was never able to find that bottle again! But Dean's deer head hangs on the cabin wall to this day, and its grin has eased many a disagreement among our teenagers through the years. When tempers would flare we'd say, "Look at Smiley!" Rising anger would cool, and that old rascal would seem to wink!

When our children were grown, the cabin again found its original purpose. With the coming of deer season, four hardy hunters come to spend their buck fever in the U.P., setting up headquarters in our cabin at Eel Lake. As they moved in, we would tell the young men, "Be sure to keep your eye on Smiley, the eight-pointer on the cabin wall."

Coming a day early, the hunters stocked the cabin with food enough for all winter and told us they were going to scout the area and tramp in the woods. I heard the ambitious nimrods discussing their "buck pole," how long it must be. There should be plenty room for four deer, but since two hunters had bow licenses as well as rifle licenses, they would probably need room for six.

Before dawn on opening day, the hunters left the cabin for their chosen stands but returned before noon without firing a shot. A strategy session followed.

John said, "We should walk and stalk the deer."

"No," Ed argued. "We must sit and post."

An early snowfall had left fifty inches of snow in the woods making it difficult to track the deer, and they weren't moving. After a good camp meal spiced with hopes and big stories, the hunters took a nap and dreamed about big bucks. Bob slept a little too long, however. When he awoke he found his friends had all gone hunting. It was almost too late, but Bob left for his hunting stand. Bob is a gentleman hunter. He knew what he was doing, too. First he prepared a comfortable seat between two young maples, neatly clearing the snow. Then he placed a patented hot pad on the seat and picked any twigs that may have fallen near his feet. Bob knew that a snapping twig would surely startle a deer and spoil a shot. Finally he sat down and waited.

Suddenly he got that feeling that he was being watched. Turning slowly, his eyes met those of a buck that wore the biggest rack he'd ever seen!

His gun! Where was his gun? His rifle still waiting for him in the cabin, Bob watched his buck taking its time trotting into the swamp, probably wondering why that man back there was rearranging the forest.

The fine buck pole near the cabin waited patiently for next season. On the cabin wall Dean's eight-point Smiley grins.

Winter

"It will take the rest of the day and all night to warm this cabin!" Claude said, shivering while starting a fire in the old iron stove.

"Why do we come here in the dead of winter?" I asked. But I know we can't resist the call of our isolated cabin on the deserted lake. We had made it again to Eel Lake, just the two of us, skiing five miles along the old forest trail. Having left the public road, all was serene, almost as if we had entered a sanctuary. Only a slight breeze whispered in the red pines near the lake.

Our Eel Lake cabin is a hiding place that challenges us to free ourselves of too much comfort, of people, even friends and family. Unpacking icy sleeping bags, I placed them on a beam over the stove where the heat rises first. Checking the thermometer I learned that the temperature was three above zero, outside and in! It was too late to drill a water hole. "I'll melt snow for coffee and hot soup," I replied, and struck a match to light the gas lamps.

"It'll be a cold night," Claude predicted. "Probably thirty below."

Huddling close to the fire, we listened to the howling wind that drove curtains of snow past our window and decided to retire early, allowing the cabin to warm while we slept. Sleeping soundly, all at once Claude shook my arm. "Amy, please, will you relax?"

"Relax?" I protested, "I was asleep! I couldn't be more relaxed."

"Probably you were having a bad dream," Claude said. "You were kicking." Then he grumbled, "There! You are wiggling your toes again. Relax!" "I'm not wiggling my toes!" I insisted. Confused by Claude's strange behavior, I tried to lie still. Suddenly wide awake, we heard a hissing and felt something move near our feet. Inspecting our heavy sleeping bag, we saw a bunch of filling protruding from a hole that told us where the intruder had entered. "It's moving! Must be a squirrel," Claude guessed. "No, it's too big," I argued, detecting a faint odor. A mink, maybe? It can't be a skunk!

By the dim light of our kerosene lamp we saw a white head with beady black eyes staring at us. A long slender white body emerged, followed by a black-tipped tail. An ermine! The creature slipped from the sleeping bag and escaped under our bed.

"He's gorgeous!" I cried, opening the cabin door. I was sorry to send him out into the cold night. Crawling once again into our cold bed, we slept, sheltered by the log walls of our cabin.

It was early morning when the snap of a mouse trap awakened me. The trapped mouse's struggle kept me awake. I comforted myself with the thought that it was the mouse that had that messed my drawer last week, but that didn't ease my guilt as I listened to the mouse dragging the trap across the floor. Then all is quiet. "What would be the time? Maybe I should add more wood to the fire. And I hated to learn how cold it was.

"Amy, why are you up so early?" Claude's sleepy voice asked. "It's 35 below," I replied. "I fed the stove."

Claude did not turn over. I sat by the stove watching the flames dance as they whispered comforting, unending words. I made coffee, enjoying the early hour and remembering the first time we saw this little cabin built against the hill. Dean Young had selected a perfect spot for his deer camp. I counted 28 cedar logs on the short wall, 38 on the long wall. Dean had cut 125 trees in his spare time to build the cabin. Now, almost fifty years later, the flames or our fire transformed the old logs into pure gold. During the day the cabin interior looks dull, but when darkness falls, the smooth cedar springs to life.

Cold, yellow dawn began to color the trees on the hills across the lake. I watched them turn to a bright orange and I realized how rich we were! It almost frightened me, for such riches are impossible to share.

The gray jays came first to the feeder, then the chickadees and nuthatches found the peanut butter stick. Later, a flock of pine siskens and grosbeaks quarreled over the sunflower seeds.

"It's time for breakfast." I called to Claude, still burrowed in the sleeping bag. Again he asked, "Why were you up so early?"

"We caught a mouse and it kept me awake." I replied.

"Oh, I heard that too," he said, "I'll check."

The mouse had escaped. Surprised that we felt relieved, we laughed.

Then we spotted our night visitor again. He was at the bird feeder chewing off chunks of suet for breakfast. "We'll gladly share breakfast with him this cold morning," I told Claude. "Fine," he replied, "But there's definitely a "No Vacancy" sign out for a bed!"

Spring

On a warm spring day the fat bluegill bulls move close to shore to make beds for the females bulging with eggs. Fighting for their territory, the angry, scrappy fish are easy to catch.

Finding a shallow place in a sheltered bay, we went crazy, those bluegills and I. The angry fish at one end of the line fought to escape, and I on the other end fought to prevent escape. Sometimes they won, but usually I was the winner.

Deciding that such a valiant fight for life must be rewarded, I determined to set the fish free, but not before showing it to my husband Claude who refuses to believe the size of my fish unless I produce the evidence. My trophy swims alongside the boat in the live net.

Though Claude does not fish, he diligently filets all I catch. I feel no guilt for his labors, for he will eat most of the fish.

Notches cut in Claude's cleaning board (he claims are one inch apart) prevent me from lying, he says. This verifies that Claude is not a fisherman: he will not lie, at least not about my fish!

Summer

Splash! Splash! Another splash. Like the frogs they catch, our nine-year-old grandsons are never dry behind the ears, and now they are racing for the "Loon Rock," screaming and hollering to see who will be first.

For our grandsons, the two days at the cabin are a continuous contest. Who catches the most frogs? Who brings home the most fish?

"There are billions of frogs, Grandma," says Patrick, "but we'll share Herm." "Who's Herm?" I ask.

"This little frog. He's funny and cute, and smiling, too!"

But when Patrick got hold of a snake, Herm was forgotten. "It's a garter snake, Grandma," Patrick informs me. "We looked it up in your reptile book. It said if you're lucky and it's a female you may have sixty snakes next year." "Sixty snakes!" Jake said. "There'll be snakes all over this place."

"We'll share her too," Patrick said, holding up his snake. "Let's put her in the pail with Herm."

Herm took a futile leap for freedom, then waited patiently to be released, now sharing his pail with a snake.

The boys had to share the outhouse, too; only a one-holer.

On hot, thirsty summer days, boys drink gallons of KoolAid, calling for frequent runs to the little house and another race.

"Hurry, Jake, Hurry!" cries Patrick. And there was no time to lift the seat, I discovered.

"Please tell those boys to use that place properly!" I ordered Claude.

"That's no problem," he replied. He summoned Patrick, Mark, and Jake, and lined them up in front of the outhouse.

"Now you fellows listen good," he said. "When you have to relieve yourselves of a simple pee, you must lift up the toilet seat. Better yet, go in the woods.

Raised in the city, the boys looked up at Claude. There was a moment of silence, then Jake said, "But you can't do it in public, Grandpa!"

"What public?" Grandpa shouted. "We don't have people living within ten miles of our lake! And stay away from the cabin, go over the hill. Grumbling something about city slickers, he headed for his shop."

Leaving for home the next day, the boys and I ran ahead of Grandpa to the car. He stayed behind to make sure all the doors and windows of the cabin were locked, and he took his time about it.

Waiting in the car, the three young men grew restless.

They found an excuse to slip outside. "Grandma, I have to go," Jake said.

"So do I," echoed Mark and Patrick.

Well, Go!" I said. Watching through the rear view mirror, I saw three boys standing in a row having another contest.

Just then Grandpa came walking out of the woods. "Did you see that?" he asked with pride, looking back at his grandsons.

"Yes, I did. They learn fast!" I replied, equally proud. "But tell the boys," I added, "Please, not in public!"

WE DIDN'T SEE ANYTHING

Claude and I haven't grown up with guns, hunting being an exclusive sport in Europe. That some one actually can pull a trigger to kill a beautiful deer has been an impossibility for me, although I recognize the need for hunting and like to eat venison. One season, however, we went deer hunting.

I asked my husband for the third time, "Are you sure that gun isn't loaded?"

Shrugging his shoulders he didn't answer me. A friend had invited us to come deer hunting on his farm in Menominee County, a new experience for us.

"A gun can be dangerous," I said, beginning to warn Claude once more and trying to get his attention.

"There's nothing to it, Amy," he replied. "I'm checking my gun, that's all."

"I'm not taking my gun," I said. "You can take yours, but I have no urge to shoot deer."

"Then, what are you doing there, going hunting without a gun?" he asked, smiling and looking somewhat superior.

Not appreciating his grin, I told him, "I'm posting. That's what they do in Carney."

Arloene Johnson called to make sure we would take warm clothing along since it could get quite cold at their farm. She said they don't do much walking but would be posting. The hunters will hide at a certain place, or post, and wait until a deer passes by.

"So you will post!" Claude said, very amused.

"Yes, with Arloene, I'll sit with her and she'll do the shooting," I told him.

"Great hunter you are," he answered. "Bertil Johnson told me he has too many deer on his land eating the corn. We may hunt for doe too. You and I have a doe permit so we'll come home with four deer if we're lucky."

Taking his gun, he went target shooting, telling me once more, "There's nothing to it. No need to be afraid!" Hearing him practice in the backyard, I shuddered, already being gun shy before the season had even begun.

We arrived in the evening at our friend's home, wearing our warm snowmobile suits, heavy wool socks and boots. Claude was carrying the one gun.

"Where's your gun, Amy?" Bertil asked.

Casually I told him, "My gun isn't good for hunting deer so I'll be posting with Arloene."

Infected with hunting fever, we women soon became as excited as they were. Arloene had prepared a delicious venison stew for supper. "For good luck tomorrow," she said.

After the meal, Bertil couldn't resist telling us a tall bedtime story about the time he shot his largest deer, a twelve point buck, killing it with one shot. That buck was standing at the edge of his cornfield as if it were waiting for him. When he got up to his deer to tag it, he was very much surprised to find not only had he killed a buck but also a doe! He said it had been difficult to convince the game warden of his double kill, although in the fall it is normal for a doe and buck to be close together. Until this day, he wasn't sure how it happened.

At five a.m. the next morning Arloene called, "Breakfast is ready!" It was still dark when our footsteps were breaking the early morning quiet and crunching the ice covered grass, hoping the deer wouldn't hear us.

We sat down in a small furrow near a cornfield. Arloene told me, "Now, we must not talk. The deer come here to feed at night and have a feast eating Bertil's corn."

He and Claude had chosen to post from a blind near a cedar swamp and were soon disappearing behind a hill. Waiting and watching, we suddenly saw the beautiful silhouette of a buck appear against a bleak gray sky. But even with the help of the new scope Bertil had given Arloene for her birthday, she had no chance to take aim as it was moving too fast toward a stand of cedars across the road. Later, two fawns darted from the cornfield, jumping like unconcerned children just having fun playing tag.

"Amy, do you want to try my gun?" Arloene asked.

"What, you want me to shoot at those cute little fawns? No! No! Let's get a big one," I said.

"Yes, they are only babies, little Bambi's," Arloene agreed. Then a doe came by with her ears twitching, carefully looking out for her fawns and giving a short snort as a warning.

"She knows that we're here," my friend whispered. "Do you want her, Amy?"

"No, no! She's a good mother. Please don't shoot her," I begged.

"Aw Amy!" Arloene said as she raised her gun reading my thoughts.

Quickly changing my position so my noisy snowmobile suit gave enough of a warning, the doe gave another loud snort, and jumping to her fawns, we saw them waving three white tails at us.

Relieved as I sat down to post again, my body seemed to solidify in the cold damp air. The wind blowing from the northeast made the dry cornstalks whisper in the sad monotonous sounds. I was beginning to feel homesick, and longed for the shelter of my home in the hemlocks.

At approximately 8 a.m., Arloene asked, "Shall we walk home, Amy, and see if our husbands have returned from their hunt?" The question could have not have come at a better time for me . I'd had enough of posting!

We asked the men waiting in the kitchen, "Did you see anything?"

"No, we didn't see anything at all," they said. But we sure got cold and are hungry and ready for a second breakfast."

Later that day, Arloene chose another location for us to hunt from; an old homestead overlooking a beautiful valley. We sat in an old milkhouse expecting the deer to come and feed in the orchard next to a caved-in barn. The old structure still showed the craftsmanship of the man who built it, the logs fitting perfectly with the corners still intact. A tumbleweed covered with frost caught in some weeds near the building sparkled in the golden sunlight, transforming it into a bejeweled crown.

Far too soon, Arloene whispered, "Here they come!"

Grazing only a short distance from the shack were two does with their fawns. Raising her gun and taking careful aim, Arloene fired her first shot. Innocent and curious at first, the deer looked in our direction, not quite understanding what happened. Then one doe took a great leap, with the others following and heading for the safety of the woods. Arloene fired once more.

Relieved to see them go, I said, "You missed, Arloene!"

"It must be my new scope," she said, but suspiciously she looked at me. "Seriously now Amy, you're not praying that I miss, are you?"

I didn't say a word.

"I'm not so sure I missed," she said. "There may be a trail of blood so let's take a walk and look."

Not wanting to see blood, not in that beautiful valley, I said again, "You've missed, Arloene. There isn't any blood here. I don't see anything."

So we left for home and returned to her bright kitchen. There the hunting experience seemed unreal. Claude had come home earlier, having had no luck. He hadn't seen anything!

Bertil, very upset, joined us later, telling us a nice buck had come across the field and just when he was ready to pull the trigger, "road hunters" had stopped and fired at his deer. They missed, but he was angry!

"Road hunters?" I asked.

"Yes, some men don't want to post or track for deer but ride the country roads shooting at anything that moves," Bertil explained. "It is illegal but it happens every year."

"We'll try again tomorrow morning. Maybe we'll have better luck," Arloene encouragingly said. "And breakfast will be ready at five a.m. Bertil, Amy and I would like to post at the cornfield again where we were this morning." Claude decided to choose the blind near the swamp and Bertil would try the shack where we had been hunting at the old homestead.

The next morning the wind had shifted and the little furrow was a cozy place for posting. Chickadees came to visit us making small talk but also may have been warning the deer of danger because we didn't see anything at all.

At 8 a.m., Arloene suggested that we take a walk across the cornfield. "We may spook a deer," she said. But again we didn't see anything so we headed for home.

Unlacing our big boots before entering the kitchen we smelled coffee. Bertil had come home before us. Dipping the dry cinnamon

121

toast in his coffee, he sat sipping it at the kitchen table. Giving us some toast too, seriously and quietly he said something to his wife. I heard Arloene answering him saying, "But we looked Bertil, and we didn't see anything!"

Listening now, I heard him say, Arloene, it was right in your sight. You shot that deer. It was a nice doe only 100 feet from that old shack. The raven made me take a look and a trail of blood led me to the carcass." Shaking his head he looked sadly at us.

Understanding why he was so upset, I remembered that this was my fault. I didn't want to see that trail of blood so I confessed, "It was me, Bertil. I'm guilty of taking a life and wasting it. Arloene was trying to find that deer but I told her she had missed." Bertil again shook his head sadly.

Claude, the last one to arrive home from his hunt entered the kitchen and we asked the familiar question, "Did you see anything?"

He told us a nice buck had come to his blind and curiously looked right at him but the deer had resembled our goat "Barbara" so much he told it, "Shsuss verdwyn!" The buck took Claude's advice and was gone in seconds.

Arriving home from the hunting trip, our hemlocks were covered with snow, as always wrapping us in the confinement of winter. It is the longest season of the year here and so much appreciated by us who love the U.P. of Michigan. Jokingly, we "U.P.ers" admit the folly of living here when all nature is groaning and protesting in -40 degree temperatures, but we enjoy the challenge.

Sitting near the open fireplace, we watched the flames dancing as they warmed and entertained us. Planning ahead for next deer season, Claude said, "I'll make a blind here in the woods. Do you remember that clearing near the creek? That is where I'll shoot my buck next fall. Nothing to it."

DEAD MAN'S HANDS

On our way to Lake Superior along the back road we pass an old house, the weathered shack of John Kivi. The house leans to the east, its walls are warped and cracking, and the sagging porch has separated itself. Folks tell us John Kivi's old house is haunted.

Indeed, on a stormy night in late fall with the northwest wind blowing naked branches against a broken window, the house near Black River looks haunted. Yet in spring when the five apple trees bloom the overgrown lilacs hide the shack, John's old home has a certain charm. Then the windows that stare blindly south sparkle as they did when John Kivi brought his Ailli there.

Together John and Ailli planted the apple trees, and a pear tree too. From her parent's homestead Ailli brought the lilac shoots but Ailli was to learn that her husband had a peculiar way of spreading love and happiness.

From the time he was a boy walking in the woods John had always heard a song. The wind in the trees stirred rhythm and melody in his head. At Black Harbor John heard music in the great waves from Canada that roared against the clay banks, and in the wavelets that lapped innocently at the Lake Superior shore. For John there was always music; happy and sad music, sometimes strange music.

On weekends John played his mouth organ as young people danced in Leppanen's barn. He kept time by stomping one foot. It was there he met Ailli. He could not dance with her, of course, for then the music would stop. But after the dance when he walked Ailli along Black River he heard music in the rapids and waterfall. When he took Ailli in his arms, he grew light headed from the happy music in his soul.

Finally John saved enough to buy the small house near Black River, and he and Ailli found joy. With borrowed money they bought a cow. Ailli's father gave them a pig and some chickens. It was enough.

Then one day Ailli missed John's handsome, red-checkered, wool Mackinaw. John told her he had traded it for an accordion and he showed her the ancient instrument. A poor thing it was, but how John could make it sing! All that summer he serenaded Ailli, and she swayed to his happy tunes though she was heavy with their first child. It would be a boy, no doubt, and then life would be wonderful in their small home near Black River.

Each night John came home singing from his work in the woods, and when supper was done, he played polkas, sometimes a hymn on his accordion. Then he would extemporize, playing tunes he had heard in his head as he worked the day through in the woods.

Content with life and with Ailli and their son, John no longer played at Leppanen's barn. He played now just for himself with his family for an audience. Two more children had come, a girl and another boy. Reluctantly John laid aside his accordion and began building an extension on the house. But even when building he sought new rhythms as he drove the nails with his hammer. The work went slowly, and Ailli, tired of the constant music, feared what the neighbors would think when John's strange, rhythmic pounding reached their ears.

The Stubbins were their neighbors, Eino and Bertha, and Ailli watched Eino tend his beautiful garden. His farm prospered; John's didn't. Ailli had to work her garden to keep the family fed. When John forgot to milk the cow, Ailli did that too. She fed the chickens and sat with the sow when it came time for the piglets to be born. Soon Ailli was expecting again.

Each day was the same. John came home from the woods and ate his supper. Then he played the music he had heard as he worked, rarely paying attention to Ailli or asking how the children were.

Like all U.P. men, John made extra wood for the needs of coming winters. One day, he loaded next year's wood on his truck and drove to town to sell it. Pleased, Ailli waited at home, for the children needed new clothes and she needed a dress. Ashamed of their faded, worn out clothing, the family had missed Sunday church several months now.

She heard the old truck turn into the yard and looked anxiously through the window. When she saw what John had bought with next winter's wood, she went to bed and cried.

John didn't notice. Proudly he carried his new accordion into the small, shabby kitchen. It was a deep-red, shiny instrument with a full keyboard and many chord buttons.

Caressing the keys, soft music filled the house, but that could not ease Ailli's tears. John poured his love into music, but long before that night, Ailli had lost her love for him.

The next morning after John had gone to the woods Ailli hung her wash out to dry. She hated the sight of the tattered rags outgrown by her three little ones. Across the clothesline she could see Eino's house and Eino at work in his garden. He looked tall and strong as he turned the rich soil, and looking up, he caught sight of Ailli. He waved a cheerful good morning and beckoned her over.

It made Ailli feel good to feel friendship. She smoothed her hair under a red bandanna and walked to Eino's garden.

As usual, Eino's Bertha had gone to town. Having no children, she often left for a day, and sometimes for a week. She liked life in town and visiting friends, while Eino was a quiet country man. He loved his land and the woods and the refreshing breeze that blew in from Lake Superior.

"Coffee?" he asked, and Ailli gladly accepted. Just to hear a man talk and listen was a wonder, and when she mentioned offhand that she hadn't yet spaded her garden, Eino said, "First we have coffee, then I'll spade that garden.

Maybe tomorrow?"

Eino came the next day to spade the garden, and Ailli fixed him coffee. And with both John and Bertha gone so much, coffee times soon became bed times.

John didn't notice. He just played his music, strange tunes that haunted his hearers. He played off-beat rhythms, odd chord combinations, with abruptly changing tempos. Then he began taking his accordion to the woods with him, and fewer saw logs came out to his clearing

One day John drove to town again, taking their last two pigs with him. Ailli waited for him to come home for supper, but finally she fed the family. She milked the cow, put the children to bed, then she went to visit Eino. Looking into her eyes, he saw how tired she was. Still, she looked so very beautiful.

Coming home late, John banged on the locked door. Ailli heard him return to the truck. In the morning she saw him, still asleep, hugging the leg of a small organ. John had sold the pigs, traded in his accordion, and bought an electronic organ. It barely fit through the door of the house, and that day John did not go to work.

So intent was he to master his new organ, he did not see Ailli leave. Soon John made great music, strange music such as never was heard by the folks in the Black River valley, or anywhere else on earth.

Not until supper time when the school bus brought the children did John notice that Ailli was gone. Feeding leftovers to the children, but not hungry himself, John played far into the darkness. Ailli slept at Eino's home that night, for Bertha, tired of Eino's quiet farm, had left for good to seek fun in town.

Obsessed with his organ, John barely missed Ailli, when she moved with Eino to a small place south of town. Eino took a job in

the mine, and it swallowed the man who loved the open spaces. Everyday he worked far underground, but knowing that Ailli waited at home made the day go faster.

At first neighbors brought food to John when they learned that Ailli had left him. A kind woman who lived alone near where the bus left the children gave them their supper and filled their lunch pails, and soon the children were hers.

At John's place the cow went dry and the fields lay abandoned. Needing money, John sold the cow and his land, and once more he went to town. He entered the music store, his face bright, almost shining, and laid his hand on the largest organ. It's reddish, warm cherry wood gleamed, and John cried, "I want this one!"

With lusting eyes John nodded to the startled salesman. "This is mine," he said in a hoarse whisper, and he paid for the organ with cash.

That day a truck brought John's organ to his house. Measuring the door with an experienced eye the delivery man said, "It's too small. The organ will never go in." John took a crowbar and ripped off the door post. The porch floor groaned under the weight of the organ as the men carried it in. They shoved the fine organ into the kitchen space, leaving barely room for its delicate bench. They noted John's burning passion to make music. "He's crazy," was their conclusion.

John fondled the white keys one by one, then the black keys, then the stops. Placing his feet reverently on the polished pedals, he began to play. For days he played, forgetting to eat, taking only brief, fitful naps. Knowing neighbors, hearing the music, brought John hot soup or sometimes a pasty.

Day after day John played his big organ, and wild melodies poured from his home. John and his organ now were one. Then one morning the music ceased. Once again the battered door post was removed, this time for his coffin.

Much later we came to our house in the woods to escape the rush of the city. We found that people in the U.P. knew each other not only by name but by their deeds, sorrows, and joys. They knew who we were, not just what we were called, and they learned that my husband Claude was a skilled organist.

Soon he was playing for vacationing church organists, and friends told us the strange story of John Kivi. His organ still rested in that haunted house along the Black River road.

For Claude, a lifelong dream came true when four strong men arrived one day. They carried John's organ into our home in the woods, and said, "Claude, play for us!"

"What do you want me to play?" Claude asked.

"Anything!" they said, "But no church stuff this time. Do you know any polkas?"

In the organ bench Claude found new sheet music which the store had supplied for John Kivi. It was evident he had not used it, John's music came from within. Claude spread out the sheets and the organ eagerly responded. Happy chords rose to the rafters of our cathedral ceiling. How the men laughed and stomped their feet! Through the open windows the music spilled into the woods around us. A robin flew to safety, and squirrels scrambled up trees. Who ever heard such noise in our forest?

When the men had gone home, a strange quiet settled down as Claude sat silently at the organ. Then his hands moved, he began to extemporize, something he rarely does. I stared at my husband. Never had I heard such music as he played then.

A perfectionist, Claude always tries to interpret the music to reflect the composer's desire. Whether classical or sacred, he seeks to echo the harmonies of God's love. Claude becomes Bach or Handel when he plays their works, but this was no sacred music! Wild, sinister, sonorous chords haunted our ceiling rafters. I listened stunned, and in my husband's drawn face I detected an intense struggle.

Suddenly he stopped and flung himself from the organ. "No!" he shouted. "I must never do that again! Those were not my hands that played such music." Shaken and pale, he stared at his hands, then buried his face in them.

BLESSED BE THE TIE THAT BINDS

The jubilant organ prelude played by my husband before the evening service at the Baptist church matched the brilliant colors of an early fall Sunday. Claude had taken the place of the regular organist who was on vacation.

Sitting in a pew near the organ that provides a view of the entrance, I recognized friends, several of whom smiled a greeting as they settled down in the seats they occupied Sunday after Sunday.

My husband's talent as an organist provides opportunity for us to worship in denominations other than our own. We enjoy the Baptist folks, especially. They are outgoing and sing with heart and soul. Their informal evening fellowship includes plenty of joyful congregational singing. Always a warm welcome is given to anyone "who enters His gates with gladness."

One Sunday, in contrast with the happy mood of the Sunday evening worshippers, seven women walked slowly into the church and sat in the last pew. With their dark polyester dresses cut from one pattern and their somber expressions, they looked like seven starlings perched on a telephone wire. Reverently and patiently, they waited for the action to begin.

As the pastor and song leader mounted the platform, my husband changed from the prelude to a familiar hymn to set the mood for the worship service. Asking the congregation to stand, the song leader balanced himself firmly and directed us in " Stand up, Stand up for Jesus!" I watched the starlings. One of them, perhaps the oldest sister, did not stand. She had entered the church ahead of the group, supporting herself with a walker.

Announcing another song, the leader again asked us to stand, and this time to smile as we sang. "Let us sing 'We Are Bound for the Promised Land'!" The hymn shook the rafters and it seemed as though everyone was ready to head for the Promised Land that instant. The starlings, not expecting so much volume from such a small group of worshippers, tried their best to join in, but they didn't smile.

Curious, I kept looking at the unusual group of women. The pastor was introduced. "Please open your Bibles to the Gospel of John, chapter 3," he said. The seven women searched the pew rack. They began to whisper and shake their heads. There were no Bibles in the racks. Baptists bring their own Bibles to church. Even little children not quite ready to read carry one, pretend to read from their picture Bibles.

The seven visitors obviously began to feel uncomfortable. Empty handed, should they focus on the pastor? He might notice that they had no Bible! I understood. On occasion I have found it difficult to follow the liturgy in new churches where Claude became organist. I remembered a time when other worshippers responded with a jubilant, unexpected Hallelujah refrain that left me totally confused. It was obvious that after their ordeal, these ladies would need a friendly greeting. So concerned was I about the ladies that the pastor's sermon was lost to me. Half way through the sermon, I noticed the older lady handing a roll of mints down the row to her sisters. Seriously listening, they did not seem to lose a word of what the pastor said. At the offertory, the older woman handed out the evening sacrifice, I imagined it would be one dollar each.

The worship ended with a hymn and prayer and Claude began a joyful postlude. The women rose and walked toward the foyer, making room for the crippled lady to move slowly from the sanctuary.

"The seven starlings," as I had privately named the visitors, were standing outside when I introduced myself. "We are happy you came to visit us tonight," I said, "I hope you enjoyed our service." I explained that my husband was the organist.

"Yes," the crippled woman said, "The service was good, and that was good singing, too. So that was your husband playing. He sure plays loud!"

"Why don't you have Bibles in your church?" she asked bluntly. "We do in our church in Grand Rapids."

"Baptist people always bring their own Bibles. That is their habit," I answered.

"Oh," she said. "Well, we are all sisters. My name is Anne. I am the oldest. And this one is not our sister, she was married to my brother, but he died, so we took her in." She named all the sisters from the oldest to the youngest. "We have never married and all live in the same house where we were born, Anne explained. "We are all Dutch."

"You are?" I said. "So am I!"

"That's what we thought, didn't we girls?" They all agreed. "You talk as if you've just come from the boat, like our Ma and Pa. You remind me of them," she said.

Laughing, I replied, "It has been over thirty years since I came from 'dat' boat, but I still talk like 'dis'!"

"How did you get up here?" Ann asked.

"We came to the U.P. to retire and to escape from the big city of Grandville near Grand Rapids," I told her.

"Well, well! " said Anne. "Then you know everything about us Dutch Reformed, aren't you? We girls are taking a vacation, always do. We are on the way to Minnesota for a color tour. Last night we took a motel in Ironwood and paid for two nights because we don't want to travel on Sunday . Early this morning we looked for a church. I don't walk well, so we looked for a church without steps."

"I am glad you enjoyed our service tonight," I said. "Come again!"

"I am not quite happy," Anne replied. "It's different from our services. You skipped the Apostles Creed too." She changed the subject. "Do you live near by?"

"We have a home in the woods near Lake Superior," I said. "Perhaps you would like to see our place and have coffee with us. It is quite a drive, though," I told her, remembering her convictions concerning Sunday travel.

"Well, girls, what do you say?" Anne asked. She turned to me,"How far is it out to your house?" she asked cautiously. "It's approximately ten miles north of here," I told her.

The seven sisters weighed the pros and cons. Finally Anne decided. "Girls, we played Scrabble all last night and this afternoon. We have been two times to church and we don't watch TV on Sunday. You want to play more Scrabble tonight! I'd say, let's go with this couple to their home for coffee."

Ann's decision left Claude out numbered eight to one and he didn't seem too happy at that moment. Following our little truck

131

closely, the sisters rode in their big Cadillac to our place deep in the woods.

"We thought we'd never get here!" Anne said. "You would not get me to live out here. Too bad you don't have neighbors."

"Oh, we have neighbors," I replied, "about two or three miles away."

"This is quite an adventure," Ann said as she eased herself into Claude's captain's chair at the table. "It's off the beaten path for us, and that on Sunday night! But it feels like home. You have a lot of Dutch stuff here; all those pretty dishes and spoons."

"We've been turned around and confused all day, haven't we girls? All because I have to go to a church without steps. This morning we were worshipping with the Lutherans. That was exercising--up and down. I could not do it, but the girls tried, and we were all nervous. The pastor did have a good sermon, but it was too short for me, and he chanted a lot. There's mostly singing in that church. Why, why that minister even chanted his prayers! And we were always behind, because they skip things in that book. No Bibles there, either. We read the Scripture from a bulletin. A nice man tried to help me, but we were all mixed up."

"Yes," I said. "My husband plays the organ there, too."

"I did not see you this morning. So you play there?" Anne asked Claude. "What are you anyway? Where do you belong?"

"We are Christians," Claude replied. " I play wherever they need me. At one time we were Reformed like you."

When the Dutch rusk with cheese and cake and coffee were placed on the table Anne was convinced we really were Dutch! "Girls, we are at home!" she commented, relieved and feeling safe, knowing she had not strayed too far. But she had one more question before being sure that this adventure was not going to turn sour. "Do you still have a Reformed Psalter Hymnal?" she asked.

"Yes, we do," Claude assured her. "Which do you like best the old red or the newer blue one?"

"The blue one would be fine," Anne said. Choosing the numbers, she asked Claude to play the organ. She directed and the sisters sang, their voices blending beautifully, reflecting the unusual love and harmony in the relationship of our visitors.

At lunch, the adopted sister, the most lively member of the

group, and I had a good discussion. "Amy, why do you think so many churches have high steps?" she asked.

"Maybe those churches with the highest steps feel closer to heaven," I said, meaning it to be a joke.

Anne had a better answer. "I wish there were no steps in front of any church so that everyone could easily walk into God's house without restrictions." That was the best sermon I had heard all day.

Looking at her watch, Anne warned, "It is ten o'clock; bedtime, girls. We still have a long drive to our motel. But it's been a wonderful Lord's day for us! Thank you for playing, Claude. God must be pleased to have you play for all these different churches. We would like to sing one more hymn. Girls, what do you say? What comes to mind?"

With one voice they chose "Blessed be the tie that binds our hearts in Christian love."

THE ZANY WOODPECKER

In our U.P. woods we often hear a soft tap tap tap, a sound lost to most people today. Even here in the quietness of the forest near Lake Superior, one must listen closely to catch the woodpecker's gently tapping as he searches the bark of a tree for food. But almost everyone is familiar with the rhythmic hammering cadenza of a woodpecker telling the world that he is happily impressing his mate nearby.

At the driveway leading to our home in the woods, a handsome woodpecker sign points the way to the house. My husband Claude carved that sign. I am a woodcarver's wife. Happily he taps and hammers away as he carves wonderful creations. My husband is a woodpecker too!

Before retiring, Claude spent a lifetime making cavities in steel for industrial dies and molds, but now he carves in wood. Compared to tempered steel, Claude says, even ironwood, our hardest northern tree, is soft.

Claude's objects of art are always of his own design. He's an original, refusing to copy anything, unwilling even to duplicate one of his own works. And he will never, never paint over wood! "The true artist is nature itself," Claude tells me.

Often I've asked Claude to carve me something practical, like a bowl or beautifully carved spoon. In our township, my friends still use wooden spoons carved by their Finn husbands or fathers, spoons that have lasted for years. I wanted one, too, but had to beg several times before Claude grudgingly agreed. When he had finished, he said, "Here is your order, Madam, but I made it only because I loved you."

Claude would much rather surprise me. Sometimes, he will make a sign from rough white cedar. His favorite wood is a slightly curved slab, which he polishes until it shines, then carefully draws his pattern on it.

Instead of simply carving letters in the wood, he chisels away

134

unwanted material to raise the name and design from the surface. People have to accept this unusual, ornamental motif, often with tree branches adding a special effect. Seeing his work for the first time, some will ask, "Did you glue those letters on that board, Claude?"

"They will have to figure that out for themselves," Claude tells me slyly.

I'm shamed to say I don't always appreciate Claude's vague, artistic ways. Often curious about a project, I ask questions and gain only obscure answers. But I will be right there in his shop when I hear his tap, tap, tap.

"Is that going to be a bowl?" I ask.

"Hmmmm," he replies.

"If that's going to be a bowl, it will not be deep enough," I tell him.

"Maybe it will not be a bowl," he says.

"You've got that off center," I warn him. "It will be a crooked thing."

"I'm not yet sure what this will be," he answers.

"You're not sure what you're making?" I ask incredulously.

"No," he says, "The wood will tell me."

At such times I find it best to avoid a collision between two quite incompatible minds, so I anxiously wait until the carving is almost finished. Even then, I irritate my artist with questions and suggestions that are probably stupid: You might consider polishing that surface; or, Are you carving a pattern on the rim? Why is the bowl tilted to one side?

"Is anything not titled in this world?" he answers.

"But it's all out of proportion," I protest. "Who will appreciate this thing?"

"Someone will," he tells me. "And if not, so what? Maybe one of our eleven children will like it."

I know one of them will. All of our children are delighted with their father's creations. As one daughter said, "We can't wait until Daddy gets very old and his art gets really crazy!"

One of his creations Claude named Longnose. It is sculptured in beautiful Osage orange wood. The finely grained piece was well cured from lying for years on Cully Gage's farm near Kalamazoo. There is a natural gloss to Osage orange, a very heavy, hard wood that is a carver's delight, and it needs no preservative.

Reactions to Longnose certainly vary when friends and visitors see it for the first time. Some begin to twitch their noses when they look at it for a while. Others seem bothered by an itch. Then, there are those who tell us they feel as though their nose is growing. Many just say "Oh," and look puzzled. A few sneeze at it. A few oddballs laugh outrageously but appreciatively, they rub Longnoses's bald pate, stroking its smooth brainless head. One person told us that looking at Longnose brought a soothing feeling like that coming from meditation.

Claude may choose wood growing on our land, but always his carvings are unique. One carving is a bowl made from native white cedar with its handle forming an oddly shaped flute. He said while carving it he was reminded of our children when they practiced to master that fine instrument.

Some of Claude's wood comes from unusual places. One day, a man brought an eighteen-by-four-inch piece from an oak beam that had been salvaged from an old hotel in St. Louis, Missouri. Claude carved a fish from that narrow beam; not just an ordinary fish, but one leaping from the waves. The carving expressed a bold, happy, contagious joy for life. People feel good when they see it.

Another day, after a good meal, Claude relaxed in his chair and said, "I've chosen a section of that beautiful Osage orange wood Cully Gage gave me and am carving a nice bowl in the form of a duck."

Later, inviting me to his shop, Claude showed me the duck bowl he was carving. It had two heads but one tail, and a large egg polished to perfection lay in the center. One of the heads, obviously the male, had its mouth wide open, seeming to announce his satisfaction and his wild love for his mate. The female was looking at her egg, seemingly surprised at what she had produced.

There is always meaning behind Claude's art, though it may be lost to the casual observer.

Many times I had admired the fierce Indianhead signs that mark points of interest in our Gogebic County. Carved from rough boards, the signs are designed to attract tourist interest. Several times I hinted that Claude should carve me one of those Indian chief's, but he always refused. "You know that I don't want to copy things, Amy," was his excuse.

Then Pete Hautalla came to our door bearing a battered old plaster Indianhead. It was huge, at least 30 inches across. Pete told us it had fallen from the wall in his restaurant. "My customers miss this guy," he said.

Pete asked Claude to make him another from wood. "I'll pay you good," he said. "Want money now?" And he took out his checkbook.

Hesitating for a moment, Claude finally agreed. For several weeks he searched for just the right slab of pine. Then he carved for many weeks, copying carefully the plaster Indian's features. Although happy with Pete's generous compensation, Claude told me, "I will never, ever copy anything again. Never!" But he did. Whether it was the fish dinner in Pete's restaurant given in appreciation for Claude's work, I don't know, but when the priest of the local Catholic church came to our table and asked Claude if he would carve him an identical copy of the Indianhead, Claude said, "Yes, Father."

Not only that, Claude decided to carve two Indianheads; one, he said, for money, the other, for love. Or was it one for God and one for Amy?

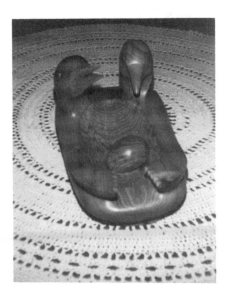

Carvings by
Claude the Artist...

THE ARTIST

Life is filled with sad paradoxes. We live joyously, almost in paradise, while others, sharing the same environment, live in deepest misery.

We are blessed, and grateful. But a short distance down our road there lived a man who was consumed by the tragedy in is life. Like us, he loved the woods and the lakes of the U.P. And he was an artist too. Let me tell his tale.

There's only one hunting cabin in the U.P. with painted murals on its inside walls. The cabin now belongs to Frank Nemecheck; the Polish Prince, we call him. He bought it from the State for back taxes. This is the story of that cabin and the man who painted the murals. He lived just down our road.

Haini Anderson turned off Lake Road onto a two-track trail that led into the woods. Gravel spit angrily at the tailgate of his four-by-four, the noise matching his mood.

Haini was nearing his hunting camp in the Upper Peninsula not far from Lake Superior. Perhaps there in the deep woods he could forget the terrible events of the last weeks and maybe find the peace and healing he so desperately needed.

At his downstate home Haini had packed as though it was deer season and he was leaving for just a few weeks as he had done so often. But it was June, not November, and he would not be returning ever. He had just buried his wife and three children who had been killed in a crash that only he had survived.

Reaching his camp on the dead-end road, it seemed to Haini that he had not been away at all, yet it was different. Where were the winter birds, the busy chickadees that always greeted him and the Canadian jays, the camp robbers?

Watching a robin scratching in the dry leaves, he said aloud, "The summer woods sure look different! Only the cabin is the same."

Haini's cabin was not like most hunting camps, the crude tarpapered shacks that pepper the U.P. forests. His was a fine log

140

and frame cabin, painted with bright colors left over from his house painting jobs down below. The camp looked more like a little house than a cabin.

It had a small front porch where Haini stored tools and other odds and ends. A larger back porch held his ax, chain saw, and hunting clothes. Haini always left his boots there before entering the kitchen.

A linoleum floor made the large kitchen feel homey when the morning sun shined through the south windows. Even when shaded by summer leaves the room was bright and cheery with its glossy white walls and red-trimmed windows and doors. Haini had always planned to move to the deer camp with his wife when he retired. Then he would remodel the cabin into a snug home for the two of them. But he did not dare think about that now, so he pretended this was just another hunting trip, a time to be alone.

Haini entered the cabin and locked the door behind him. He wanted no visitors, not even the Fredricksons who lived a mile down the road. Tom and Laura Fredrickson farmed a small homestead. They were bird watchers and loved the woods. Although it wasn't likely they would come, Tom might wonder who was at Haini's camp this time of the year. But if he spotted Haini's pickup and found the cabin door locked, he'd get the message. U.P. people know if they're needed or not.

For a long time Haini sat at the kitchen table and stared at the blank white wall. Now the whiteness reminded him of the hospital emergency room where his family lay dying. Why had only he survived?

"No!" Haini said aloud, "I must change my thinking, try to forget. But how? I need a good cup of coffee. Maybe I will prime the pump."

The clatter of the pots and pans made the kitchen seem more lively as Haini prepared a simple supper. On the table he placed one cup, one plate, and one fork. There should have been five. Again Haini spoke aloud. "What am I doing here alone in the sticks? Why did I quit a good job and sell the house so soon? All I see here are trees, trees, and more trees. What am I living for?"

Finishing supper, Haini lifted the water kettle that was singing on the stove and rinsed the few dishes. He stared at the sink. "That's all. I've finished already. Now what?"

Seated at the table, Haini put his feet on a chair and filled his pipe. He watched smoke rings drift toward the ceiling and began to feel the familiar comfort of home. "I must fix this place up," he said. "I've lots of time, and there's much to do before winter."

Again Haini stared at the white kitchen walls. "All my life I've wanted to paint pictures, nature pictures. That's what I'll do during the long winter months. Painting will keep me busy."

Unloading his truck, Haini found the supplies he had collected when he took an art course at the college the previous winter. There were tubes of delicate colors, brushes, and a palette smeared with dried paint. Now he was glad he had taken the art class.

Through the summer months Haini kept busy repairing the cabin. He checked the chimney for leaks and patched the roof. He cleaned a mess in the attic the squirrels had made. He planed the windows and doors for a tight fit against the cold that was coming, and remembering his cold feet during deer camp, Haini crawled under the cabin and insulated the floor.

Then there was wood to be made, lots of wood. He stacked a huge pile near the back door of the cabin and a pile farther back to air dry for another year. He'd need lots of wood for heating and cooking.

Arriving at the cabin in late June, it was too late to start a garden, but one day when he came home from town he found a bundle of sweet william plants on his back step. Knowing that Laura Fredrickson liked flowers, Haini figured the flowers were from her. So far, he had not even talked to his neighbors. People didn't seem to make sense anymore. Only when he went to town did he hear a human voice. What was there to say? He was alone he had to be alone. But gratefully he planted the sweet williams around his cabin.

Haini knew the Fredricksons wouldn't intrude, but if he needed help, they would be there. The sweet williams were their way of letting him know. Later, a bundle of apple tree seedlings was waiting on his step. These he planted too.

The brilliance of fall stirred Haini to take long walks, and at times the beauty of the forest almost made him forget the deep ache he carried. Slowly he was healing, but winter was coming and deer hunters would invade his woods, disturbing his dream world.

On one of his last autumn walks Haini noticed bear tracks leading to the animal's winter den. To a good woods-man like Haini, the tracks were a sign that there would be lots of snow, and soon. The sign was right. In a few days the temperatures plunged and snow fell for three days. All of a sudden it was winter, and a snow drift crept halfway to the cabin eaves.

Confined indoors, Haini grew restless. One day he said to the kitchen walls, "I'm ready. Let's go! Don't you worry, Esther, we'll make it." He had been talking to Esther a lot lately, silently at first, then aloud. It seemed to bring her closer.

Three feet of snow and below zero temperatures did not prevent the hunters from coming. Noting smoke curling from Haini's camp, they honked as their pickups plowed past. But Haini did not wave. He spent long hours staring at the white kitchen wall remembering his wife and children.

Esther had made a fine family photo album. How he wished he had kept it! Again and again he chided himself, why had he so quickly disposed of his things? Suddenly Haini felt terribly alone .

Late one afternoon the sun playing in the branches of the old spruce cast a shadow pattern on the kitchen wall. For an instant Haini saw a lake with sunlight dancing on its waters. "Esther! Did you see that?" But only the wind replied.
He must save that vision! Hastily, Haini laid out his brushes and paints. "I'll draw that lake; it's Spirit Lake. I've always wanted to build a cabin there for the boys. There's good fishing, too."

Feverishly he painted, hardly stopping to eat. The wall became a window opening onto a summer lake. On its shore he would paint his sons so he could hold them forever. Throughout the dark days of winter Haini labored. He painted the lake, then his sons, the older boy, John, and the younger, Dave. He painted them fishing for northern pike among the weeds. As he painted, Haini talked to his sons. "John, look at me. Hold up that big fish. Keep your head up, don't look at the fish. That's right. Dave! Did you get a strike?"

"That kid has no patience, Dad," John protested. "He's too small to catch a big fish."

"You must help him, John," Haini replied.

The painting was almost finished, but Haini was not happy with his work. He made change after change. He could not bear to see

143

the painting completed. Several times he tried to paint the forest stretching north toward Lake Superior, but it wouldn't come out right. He added cattails and brightened the clouds as the sun set on the shore of his small lake. Loons! The lake should have a pair of loons. He heard their wild, eerie cry.

Haini watched his sons playing on the shore and felt depressed, for the picture was almost finished. "John," he called, "Would you like a boat? Can I trust you and your little brother fishing from a boat?"

"Aw, don't worry, Dad," John replied. "We're good swimmers."

Haini was now enjoying such conversations daily. He painted the boys fishing from a small wooden boat. "Boys," he shouted across the water, "you're ready to catch that big one. When he hits, count to thirteen, then set the hook and wear him out!"

The picture was finished and Haini sat staring at it. Now what?

"We must build a cabin," he told the boys. "Where should we build it, John? Close to the waterfalls?"

Haini had painted a stream with a waterfall tumbling over grey granite rocks not far back from the lake. He imagined a brown log cabin and the boys helping him build it.

"The waterfall is a good place to take a shower," he told the older boy. "Remember the time we camped at Au Train Falls? And how we slid down the slippery rocks wearing out the seats of our swimming trunks?"

Haini chuckled at the memory and John laughed too. "Mom told us she was not going to buy us a new pair!" Their laughter echoed in the empty kitchen.

"You're not finished yet," he warned as the boys drifted toward the lake. "We must make lots of wood for winter."

"Aw Dad, we want to go fishing! Can't we?" Davey begged.

Haini sighed, "OK, go fishing, but be home in time for supper."

For a long time he sat staring at his mural on the wall. Suddenly Haini stood up. "Where are my boys? Are they really dead?" No, there was the lake, the boat, and his sons. They'd be back soon. Smiling and content, Haini slept in his chair, waiting.

Christmas came and Haini found a small gift on his step, baked goods wrapped in a new red bandanna handkerchief. He ate Laura Fredrickson's cookies and fruitcake, saving one cookie for each of his boys. Then he fell asleep on the day bed with the kerosene lamp casting flickering shadows. Suddenly he heard his little girl Anne singing a simple tune. Twinkle, twinkle little star. No! It must be the wind in the old spruce. Her voice seemed to fade, then he heard it again. Could it be the wind blowing down from Lake Superior?

With his eyes still closed, he saw her. She stood among the flickering shadows in her light blue nightgown. "Peek a boo, Daddy," she cried, her eyes sparkling. Then she was gone. Was it a dream?

Haini shook himself and put more wood in the stove. But he could not bear to let Anne go. He must paint her too. Rushing for his tubes and brushes, he set a match to the gaslight and all night he painted his little daughter on the smooth wall between the living room windows.

"My little angel, please stand still," he begged. "Don't go away from me again." Soon his Anne became real, hidden there among the cattails near the lake shore. "Anne, come to Daddy," he called and stretched out his arms to catch her and felt her small body snuggling close.

With the first light of dawn his dream faded, and Haini's vision blurred. Somehow he made it to his bed and slept fitfully until late afternoon. Finally he awoke and hurried to see what he had painted in the night. He began to laugh hysterically and could not stop. "That's not my little girl! It's a deer, a buck! I painted a buck last night."

Trembling and sobbing Haini cried, "Where's my little girl? Where's my Anne?"

Eating a bowl of leftover stew, Haini found his boys waiting for him in the kitchen. "Your little sister came last night," he told them. "She's a little angel. Don't you ever tease her!"

Haini now talked constantly to his sons, telling them where to fish, how to catch the big pike lurking in the deep hole near the waterfall. At night he lay in his bed waiting for his Anne to part the curtains and play peek-a-boo again. Once he heard her ask, "Daddy, where is my mommy?"

"She'll soon come home, honey," he answered. And turning his head to the drab bedroom wall he wept, calling her name over and over. "Esther, Esther."

The yellow gaslight cast the shadow of his outstretched arms on the wall behind his bed. "Esther, my dear love," he whispered. Sometimes she answered, and recognizing her warm, familiar voice, he waited for her to come.

Finally she asked, "Why don't you paint me too, Haini? Then we all could be together forever."

Yes! If Esther were here, his family would be complete!. Wandering from the living room to the kitchen, Haini asked himself where would she like to be. Close to the boys? No, she would want to be with him in the living room where he slept. "Mom will come and live with us again," Haini called to his boys, and he began measuring the drab wall next to his bed.

This time he would make a real painting on canvas left from his art class. He would frame it with beautiful wood.

Again he heard her say, "Forever, Haini." Remembering her beauty, her soft auburn hair, and the warmth of her supple body, he brought his love back as he had known her, and he knew she was waiting for him.

How slowly his brush moved as he worked day after day, and at mealtime he talked with his boys as they played at Spirit Lake.

One evening little Anne peeked from between the curtains and Haini asked, "Are you happy your Mommy is coming home?" Anne's eyes danced. Soon the family would be whole again.

At last Haini's masterpiece was finished, but during the day he could not bring himself to look at it. Never! Yet he could hardly wait for darkness to fall when his Esther would be waiting for him.

She was real now, and immersed in his fantasy, the winter passed swiftly and happily. Then on a spring afternoon when the earth was smelling of new life and love, Haini did not wait for night. Impatiently he undressed and lay down on his bed, hunger raging within him.

"Come Esther," he cried, and he reached out for her, but his hands brushed only rough canvas on the wall. He felt her deathly cold body and his winter-long dream shattered. Haini fled from the cabin, screaming and half naked.

Laura Fredrickson was picking spring dandelion greens in front of her house when she saw Haini run past her driveway to where the road ends in a cedar swamp. Calling Tom, they followed and found

Haini wild-eyed and babbling, lying under a windfall near Spirit Lake Creek.

They dressed the poor man and brought him in their old pickup to a doctor in Ironwood. He had seen other men go berserk in their lonely winter cabins. He advised that Haini should be cared for in Newberry, a place for men like him. But at Newberry there are no paints or brushes for a man who lost his family.

Frank Nemecheck now owns Haini's deer camp in the U.P., the one that is decorated with murals. Frank bought it for back taxes. It cost Frank very little, but it cost Haini everything.

LITTLE GIRL'S POINT

Our children who live on the East and on the West coasts will make an yearly pilgrimage to the U.P. as do all the others. We're glad not all ten of them come at the same time. The house is roomy without walls between kitchen dining area and living room, but all the shoes blocking the entrance can be too much.

Suitcases and duffel bags cram the two small bedrooms. The children claim the space in the loft. Others may set up a tent in the backyard. But strange noises in the woods often lead to a scattering of grandchildren's bodies on the living room floor in the morning.

Claude and I sleep on the hideabed in the couch, yielding our bedroom to guests who sleep longer. Our only quiet time is drinking a cup of coffee on the deck early in the morning. Quiet, that is, until some of the grandsons choose to splash in the pond or take a bath in the Finnish Sauna.

Claude fires up the sauna every morning in summer and winter, and the Sauna is preferred by all our guests. We have a shower, but with so many mouths to feed, it becomes a pantry.

A picnic at Little Girls Point takes some pressure off during the day when the grandchildren hunt for agates, returning with pockets full of stones to be sorted on the deck.

We miss each family when they leave, and shed secretly a tear, then comfort each other by saying how grateful we are for family.

Sometimes the parents allow one of the children to stay for a while, and that's what I enjoy most.

> *Listen! spirits of the greenwood plume,*
> *Shed around thy leaf perfume,*
> *Such as springs from leaf of gold*
> *Which thy tiny hands unfold.*
> *Spirits thither;*
> *Spirits repair.*

My granddaughter Cairn and I read that poem beneath the Legend of Leelinau carved in white pine on the marker by Lake

148

Superior at Little Girl's Point.

The legend told about Leelinau, the daughter of a hunter who lived with her tribe at Kaug-wudjoo near the crouching Porcupine Mountains that lie to the east. Not far from the village was a sacred grove, the place now called Little Girl's Point.

Leelinau loved to visit the dark grove of tall white pines, even though the elders had warned her that the little men of the woods, the <u>Puc Wudganees</u>, were to be feared. When angry, they might hurt a little girl.

But Leelinau was not afraid. The grove grew on Manitowak, a point that protruded far into Gitchee Gumme, giving her a beautiful view of the islands to the west. She came often, accompanied by her lover to see the sun set.

Early on her wedding day, Leelinau came to the grove. Suddenly, she disappeared! Caught away in a flaming torch. So said the legend. Old fishermen say they have seen her on misty evenings and mornings walking on the shore hand in hand with a handsome young man.

"That's how Little Girl's Point got its name," I told Cairn.

"It would be such fun to camp here!" she replied. We often come here to picnic or watch the sunset, but just once I would like to see the sun rise over the lake."

Cairn's words echoed a wish that had often been mine since we live just five miles down the road from Lake Superior. I smiled at my granddaughter. "Grandpa would say that camping here would be just like kids camping in their back yard."

"But Grandma, your back yard is not Lake Superior! Please?"

I reflected a moment. Like Leelinau, I had been drawn to the great lake. The waters might be dark and foaming with whitecaps, or blue and still; but its expanse forever changing always lifted my spirits. One weary, confused day as I came to the lake, a rainbow arched its bright colors above the dark clouds and gray waters and I was renewed and cleansed and at peace.

The Indians understood that feeling, for here they had established the sacred grove where they sacrificed to the Great Spirit. Now the tall pines sheltered picnickers and campers. I had often envied vacationers camping at the park. When I said to Cairn, "We'll ask Grandpa if he will help us set up our tent," she was overjoyed.

When we told our plan to Claude, he replied as I expected that he would rather sleep in his own bed. Perhaps, though, he'd visit us for a good camp meal.

So Cairn and I chose the last campsite on the ridge with a wide view of the lake and facing the Porcupine Mountains to be far from other campers. Later in the evening after the tent was pitched and a fireplace made, Cairn and I hiked far down the beach, picking up polished, bright-colored stones hoping to find agates. Then we gathered driftwood for our evening campfire pretending that each bleached, gnarled piece was the bone of a prehistoric animal, perhaps a dinosaur, that had washed to shore long ago.

Fifty of my many years vanished. I was a teenager again, imagining with Cairn that wild beasts lurked behind each tree. Silently, we watched the red sun disk disappear in the blue haze on the horizon. Darkness fell swiftly over the lake and Cairn said, "Now we must remember to see it rise in the morning, Grandma."

One by one the stars appeared as we huddled close to our campfire. Cairn whispered, "I haven't ever seen the stars so bright! Do you see them sparkling in the lake, Grandma?" Dragging her sleeping bag from the tent, she added, "It would be fun to sleep under the stars tonight." I joined her and soon she slept soundly.

I sat by the fire and listened for a long time as the waves talked and babbled endlessly on the rocks. I Looked up at the sky, trying to identify the constellations my father had pointed out on our nightly walks in Holland so long ago. The Big Dipper reflected from the still waters of Lake Superior as it had from the North Zee. Then I too slept.

I stirred about dawn. A breeze swirled plumes of fog over the still lake. Was I dreaming? Amidst wisps of fog, two figures seemed to slip along the shore, a girl and a young man. They danced in the mists so gracefully they seemed to be one! Full of sleep and shivering I watched them dance to the rhythm of the waves, two lovers, forever one in Leelinau's sacred grove. Then the first flash of sun and they were gone.

"Grandma, was that real?" I heard Cairn whisper.

"I thought you were sleeping!" I replied.

"No, I'm not sure what woke me. I was a bit chilly. Did we see Leelinau dancing on the shore with her lover, Grandma?"

Wet with dew we dragged our sleeping bags to the tent and fell sound asleep. When the sun appeared fully , Grandpa came and I gave him breakfast and coffee.

Cairn hugged Claude and said, "Grandpa, why don't you dance on the shore with Grandma like Leelinau and her lover did? You're still in love, aren't you?

Grandpa grinned and took another sip of his coffee. "Not here in public," he said. "When I look at your grandma my eyes dance, but my legs don't cooperate."

Lake Superior

WE BELONG HERE

Our grandchildren ran ahead along the sandy beach to the mouth of a small creek. The creek seemed too tired to finish its course to Lake Superior, and it sprawled there, forming a perfect swimming pool for children.

I lay down on the warm sand to rest. The cries of happy children would not bother me, but then a mother began to lecture a small boy, "No! Jimmy, don't throw sand!"

"But mom, she splashed me first."

Sensing the issue would not soon be resolved, I casually walked down the beach and found a rocky ledge. I bathed luxuriously in the sun and listened to the waves.

"Nonsense, nonsense, nonsense," they said quietly.

"What nonsense?" I asked.

"That's right! That's right. Nonsense," the waves replied. They spoke in short sentences, as good friends do who need but a few words to understand each other.

I lay peacefully on the hot sand with a hugh rock for a back rest. The sky was bright blue. It was very still, save for the waves' low murmur. The rock was strong, like God. I was a grain of sand fallen from the rock, drawing wisdom from the waves. "That's right, that's right! People nonsense." I felt myself one with the land and lake, perfectly at rest.

After a time I looked up. Claude came walking down the beach and I returned to the world of people. He joined me, leaning against my rock.

"Did you sleep?" he asked.

"No, just rested. I talked with the waves."

"You always talk with waves, and with trees," Claude said.

"Everything has a language," I told him. "That big pine at Eel Lake speaks, but more often, it makes music, like you on the organ. The birch and aspen, they talk like me. Frogs talk and sing only when warm and content."

Claude nodded patiently.

152

"But I like loons best," I continued. "They express anger and worry, love and joy; just like people."

Claude smiled at me. "You belong here, Amy. I Would be lonely up here without you. You help me see and hear nature's secrets."

A thought crossed my mind. "When we must part someday, Claude, you must return downstate to be near the children. They will love you."

"Why do you say that?" Claude asked startled.

There was no need to answer. I understood. Claude loves the U.P. as much as I. We belong here, both of us.

Amy J. Van Ooyen and her husband, Claude
are retired and are living in Michigan's
Upper Pennisula.

Copies of this book can be
procured from bookstores in the U.P. or
by writing

Amy J. Van Ooyen
N13508 Partridge Road
Ironwood, Michigan 49938

$11.95 including postage within U.S.